HOW NOT TO FUCK-UP YOUR KIDS

WAYNE LEE

How Not to Fuck-up Your Kids
Copyright © 2018 by Wayne Lee

Editor: Hannah Gold – www.soulwriterscafe.com
Cover design: Andrea page - www.thelittlepixelhouse.co.uk
ISBN 978-1-9999630-4-0

TABLE OF CONTENTS

1.
INTRODUCTION

Being a father of two children most certainly does not give me enough knowledge to write a book on parenting. However, my career as a highly perceptive intuitive healer has given me a unique perspective of what happens when emotionally unaware parents raise children. In my practice, I help adults heal their inner-child wounds and repeatedly see the same trauma, fear and anxiety being played out. This trauma is often derived from childhood when they were raised by mostly caring, but misinformed parents.

One thing you'll soon notice about me is that I like to swear, especially on subjects I am so passionate about! Raising emotionally healthy and fulfilled children is something I am deeply committed to and so with that in mind, having seen so many fucked up adults, this book contains all my conclusions from my work as an intuitive healer and is designed to offer you alternative ideas and awareness about bringing up children. My aim is not to judge your parenting skills or to tell you what to do, but hopefully to inspire a different upbringing so your children do not have to grow up to become unstable, unhappy, fearful, un-skilled, emotionally immature older children, but rather be genuine, courageous, and emotionally mature adults.

I know that sounds a tough call. But in our day and age, with the amount of information and help out there, there is simply no longer an excuse for parents to raise children in the same way that maybe you were raised. The world has changed and as a result, we have to change the way we raise our children. Let's give an example - screen time, i.e., using TV, tablets and phones to distract your kids. Just because they're available doesn't mean we have to do it. We all know that's not great parenting; some would even go as far as to call it neglect. So, I wanted to write a book that helps you in modern-day society.

Why the need for yet another parenting book, I hear you ask, and what makes this one so special? To understand the needs of our children let's look at how they evolve. Our subconscious mind is created under the age of three years old, and then until around seven this is embedded and strengthened through repetition. As the child comes out of the subconscious development it slowly gains more and more consciousness and self-awareness as an individual and less and less awareness of their own subconscious mind. What this means is when they become adults all the good and bad behavioural lessons that were learned in childhood are at play and essentially you become the adult version of the three to seven-year-old. Or in other words, a lot of parents, unintentionally, do the most fucking up of our children before they are seven.

The aim of this book is to avoid that scenario, and to give parents the skills your children need to be outstanding progressive adults.

I know we all want the best for our child, but as a parent, it's almost impossible to be aware of all the negative patterns you are creating in your children. That's why this book will give you ideas and methods to potentially stop fucking up your kids, so they can become even more outstanding emotionally aware adults.

I know this sounds strong, and I did mention my propensity to swear when I get passionate, but the truth is simple and stark. In my mind, there is simply no excuse to not be looking at your parenting skills. There is no excuse to not be exploring and using alternative methods of understanding, seeing and being a parent. Why? Because the simple matter is when we put too much pressure, fear or expectation on a child under the age of seven, all we end up doing is creating negative, disruptive processes that only hinder that child later in their adult life. By putting pressure on them, we create dangerous incongruences in their confidence levels because their child brain is not developed enough to hold this level of pressure. Their brain will not even come close to understanding it. Do not expect your children to understand at the same level as adults.

Do not expect your child to understand you. Read that again. You cannot expect your child to understand you, even if they say they do! They are telling you what you need to hear to make you happy and keep they safe. Your child's brain is not yet developed enough. Your kids are not ready to be adults yet, not at three not at seven and not at

sixteen. A seven-year-old boy is not old enough to be responsible for anything other than hopefully lifting the seat
when they pee, so do not expect them to be the man of the
house. A seven-year-old girl is barely old enough to look
after her plastic dolly; she is not old enough to look after
her baby sibling in any way at all.

So, what's the alternative?

I believe it's far healthier to raise children within a family rhythm that puts no heavy expectation on them under
the age of seven. As they get older, then slowly you can
start to increase the expectations on them depending on
the child's confidence at home. From this point, you can
gently start to put processes into their lives, so the child
may develop further. I am not saying at seven-years-old
your child is now responsible for cooking dinner, but they
can have a chore of emptying out the dishwasher on their
own. In this example, be mindful not to make them feel in
trouble for putting things away wrong or forgetting to finish. Simply show them where things go or help them finish
over and over again without getting frustrated. (I can hear
you saying not bloody likely - but at least try it.)

Under the age of seven the child should be welcomed
into the flow of the family, allowed to help and do, allowed
to go and play, allowed to be distracted and allowed to be
a free child without any expectations for adult responsibil-
ities. At this age, the child brain is open and ready to receive and you give them the gift of learning without
pressure. You also show them how to learn and how to fit
in, even if that's just fitting in with their family, so they get
used to being in flow with their surroundings. You show

them how to grow up without a fear of being themselves. They learn from watching you do things over and over again.

I often ask clients who are parents, or are dealing with difficulties in their relationship with their parents, what they think the job of a parent is? At this early point, I think it's important to put my point of view across. Of course, I do not expect everyone to agree with me, but this has never been wronged by any of my clients and this point of view is the whole ethos of this book.

It's my belief that the job of a parent is to guide a baby, toddler, child and teenager through life, so they learn the skills to survive in the world we live in now, not in the past, now. The parent should do this through action, not words. The parent should be the positive role model that the child can learn from. The parent is NOT responsible for making the child happy. The parent is responsible for teaching the child that all of their emotions are valid, warranted and allowed, thus giving the child emotional stability in their lives. For a parent to do this they first have to be able to deal with their own emotions – to be able to hold them when they are in flow and to try not to leak their un-processed adult emotions and fears onto their children. I have seen too many people who are afraid of spiders because either their mother or fathers are afraid of spiders. Clients who do not eat certain foods because their parents do not eat them. As a parent you have to hold back your stuff, so your children do not become miniature clones of you running the same trauma time and time again. A parent's job is to raise your children to be more than they are.

Many times in my career I have had to help a client learn that it's fine for them to be more successful, more powerful, more emotional and more intelligent than their parents. Just last night I was working with a client who realized she was trying to be as successful as her mother but was also afraid of becoming more successful than her. On some deep level, she felt she would be in trouble if she outgrew her mother. During the session we discovered how afraid of her mother she'd been throughout her entire life. How this fear had caused her to procrastinate and to hold herself back from her own natural success.

This book is not rocket science and you may not agree with everything I say or even the language I use. As you've probably guessed I'm someone who is not afraid to hold back from what I'm thinking and that doesn't come from being judgmental or having a go at your parenting skills. It comes from having worked with thousands of fucked up adults over the years and the simple knowledge that so much of their problems could have been avoided with better parenting!

Therefore, this book comes from a passionate belief that to help our children grow to be the best they can be, you look at your parenting, take responsibility for your own emotions and help your child to grow up to be the best they can be. Within the following pages are some simple common-sense ideas that I have learned in my healing practice. I wish my clients had experienced the kind of parenting I'm going to teach you and the kind of parenting I try and instil in my own children as they grow up.

All I ask from you is the following: I ask you to feel into it, I ask you to decide for yourself if these ideas work for you and I ask you to take responsibility and look deep within at how you want to raise your children.

This book is focused on ideas for children under eight years old. After eight it's another story entirely.

Brace yourselves.

2.
PUTTING LOVE FIRST

As parents it's easy for us to get lost in what our children are getting wrong, where they are not doing well and what they do that irritates us. Let's face it; being a parent is hard work. It's tiring and challenging and many of us feel overwhelmed throughout the whole process with the need to constantly put our children before our own needs.

Due to the repetitive nature of parenting, you often spend all day saying no to your kids. 'Don't do that!' 'Stop that!' 'Get away from that!' 'No, that's dangerous." What?' 'What?' 'What?'

However, when we do this we end up creating a far more negative connection with our children than we intended to, and it's probably something we are not even aware of. And, even if you are aware of this negative connection, what can you do to change it?

It's so easy to get lost in the responsibility of being a parent and all the weights and concerns that brings. But being lost in this responsibility can bring its dangers. From my healing practice, I see parents who do not realize the connection they have with their children is often one of fear, frustration and aggression.

'Arrggghhh! I told you not to touch that 10 times today already!

'Arrggghghghgh! I just told you not to do that!'

'I've said it three times in the last two minutes and you still did it, whyyyyyyyyy?!!!!!!!'

Repeated statements like this from parents can have a negative effect on your children. From an early age, we inadvertently start to install the idea that they are responsible and they are to blame for making us behave with aggression, anxiety and sadness. Instead of us taking the responsibility, what happens is that *they* end up holding all our happiness on their tiny inexperienced shoulders. Our children then take on these beliefs into their subconscious and it becomes normal for them to have aggression, anxiety and negativity in their lives. As adults they will often have an uncontrollable subliminal need to recreate the normal behaviour of their childhood, a childhood that was programmed into their subconscious. Thus they might then feel aggressive, negative and be overly anxious about life.

When your child has done something which is unproductive or could hinder them or others, or they exhibit a behaviour which is not going to help them in their lives, you need to be able to address this in a way which doesn't involve aggression or negativity. Instead, install a positive learning experience by putting love first. You do not need to scare them, punish them, hurt them, manipulate them or teach them the tough lesson.

You can, and must always, put love first when you are parenting and connecting to your children. Yes, you will have bad days; you are human after all. Yes, you will have frustrating moments. Who doesn't? Yes, you will want to rip your hair out many times! But if you can allow your emotions to be love based, rather than led by fear, anger or stress, then your intention will get through to the child quicker. The child will learn to work with you, instead of becoming an obedient slave, or a robotic emotionless blob that is afraid to do anything just in case their parent gets angry.

Here's an example to illustrate what I mean:

Parenting Through Anger:

Four-year-old Andy is playing with his glass of water at the table. He is not particularly hungry and is distracted from eating his dinner by the movement of the water.

'Andy stop playing with your glass you might tip it over,' says his mum.

Andy does not hear her as he is too focused on the water moving about.

A few minutes later and mum is getting increasingly more frustrated. 'Andy, I said stop playing with your glass.'

But Andy is still too focused on the movement of the water. It's beautiful and mesmerizing to him.

'ANDY!' shouts mum in frustration.

Andy jumps at the noise and knocks over the glass and water washes over the table.

Mum is now at peak anger. 'Andy how many times have I told you! LOOK what you have done. Why don't you listen to me?'

In this very common situation, all Andy hears is the following: I am a bad boy, I am bad, I am bad, I am wrong, it's not safe to be creative, it's not safe to see the beauty in life.

Sadly, this is a common situation that happens in many different ways in many different families. However there is another way:

Parenting Through Love:

Four-year-old Andy is playing with his glass of water at the table. He is not particularly hungry and is distracted from eating his dinner by the movement of the water.

'Andy stop playing with your glass you might tip it over,' says his mum.

Andy does not hear her as he is too focused on the water moving about.

A few minutes later his mum calls his name and waits calmly for Andy to pay her attention.

He still does not hear her as he is in flow with the water and his brain is absorbing the beauty and the movement. In this present moment he is busy developing a deep creative connection.

So she places her hand gently on to Andy's arm and says calmly, 'Andy please looks at me?'

Andy looks up.

'Andy,' she says patiently, 'I love you, but I need you to listen to me. That glass may fall over and spill water all over the table. Can you stop tipping it about please?'

Andy is feeling a bit hurt, but he puts the glass down.

But because his mum is talking to him openly and with love, he feels safe to communicate with her, and so he starts to talk to her about the water.

'Mum, I like the way the water moves.'

Since his mum has created a loving situation that is open for both her and Andy to have a conversation about water, this now represents a great opportunity for them to learn about water and each other.

Mum now knows Andy is interested in movements, the flow of water and she might even consider putting him at the sink to watch the water flow down the drain.

What Andy has learned is invaluable. He can be himself without fear. He can be heard, he can be seen and he knows his mother has interest in him and his life.

For this to be able to happen a few things need to be pointed out. Firstly, these kinds of conversations happen in my life with my kids all the time. They are not just a concept. But, and here's the important bit, before they could happen, I had to work on my own issues around being heard.

As a child, I wasn't heard, so this was an area of my life I had to work at, I also had to work through any issues about being in authority. As I never had a say in my childhood I had stuff around authority I needed to process and heal. The benefit of doing this work on myself means my kids are not usually afraid to talk to me about their things. Sometimes, when I am in a grumpy mood, they may steer clear of me for a short while. Like any human, I cannot always be in that clear loving energy, but I try as much as possible. But if I have not been approachable when my kids come to me, then I will go to them when I am ready. The television show I am watching is never more important than me hearing my kids.

However, and I am the first to admit this, it's hard to change the way you deal with your kids, because you first have to deal with the programming hard-wired into you from your own childhood.

It took me months to work out the right language to use in my parenting. The language, or right words, is not going to work unless you're willing to put love first. That's easy, they are your kids. You do love them, even if that love is full of frustration at times. It is OK to huff and puff in frustration and say something like 'I love you Andy, but I'm getting frustrated that you're not listening to me.' It is OK for you to be an emotional, flowing human being.

Here are some words and phrases I use to connect positively with my children. Feel free to use them or adapt or make up your own. The only criteria is that they come with love.

Words:

"I love you, but I'm feeling very angry that you decided to do that. That was not a good choice."

"I love you, but that behaviour is not acceptable. "

"I love you, but that choice was not the best choice to make. Let me help you understand why not. Can you try it this way next time please?"

"I love you, but eating old food off the floor is unhealthy." (This one I have said very many times, over and over again.)

"I love you, but it's not ok for you to hit or hurt your sister. Come to me and tell me what's going on and I'll try my best to understand what you need. "

"I love you, but that cannot happen again as it's not fair on anyone else for you to do that. Let me explain to you why."

"I love you, but you cannot have any more sweets today. It's not healthy for you, OK, one more and that's it. "

To be able to tell your child phrases like 'I am getting frustrated';

'I am getting really stressed out at the moment about this'. 'Let's just stop and catch up', 'let's just sit down and laugh about it' is a very big step away from phrases like, 'you're making me frustrated', 'you're getting me really stressed', or 'you're making me angry'. When you say those kinds of words what you're really saying is 'you're making me feel my feeling and that's bad' instead of owning what you feel. Read these words carefully.

Instead of blaming your child for making you feel a certain way, you must own your emotions. Yes, you will not get this right all the time. It would not be human to expect you to be perfectly calm and loving all the time. Actually, I think it would be unhealthy.

Here is a universal law that not many people are aware of: when you blame someone for anything, it means you are not taking responsibility for your part. So, when you blame a child for your stress, you are not taking responsibility for yourself and instead you're putting that on your child, on a baby, on a toddler, on a kid. You are obviously not holding it for yourself, so imagine how your child will feel about holding it for you; they will be afraid, scared, overwhelmed and lost. They have no idea how to hold onto these kind of powerful negative emotions, but they will blame themselves, if you let them, and they will take on your trauma for you. They have no choice, after all, you are their survival. Their life depends on the perfect parent. They will become the bad child instead of you becoming the intolerant, bad parent who will get them killed.

You do not have to be the boss all the time, you are allowed to make mistakes, you are allowed to cry, you are allowed to have a bad day, but when you are on the other side, you can also go to your child and tell them what's going on for you and you can talk to them. They may not understand your words, but they will understand your connection and your love, they will understand that even when things are feeling uncomfortable they do get better. They will learn to get over things with love and connection and not to be afraid of you, your emotions or themselves.

Throughout this book you may notice me pointing out one simple concept. In fact, I'll keep on repeating it, just like I am talking to a child. If you want to be the best parent you can be, learn to deal with and hold your own emotional space. Be courageous and own your stuff.

Putting love first starts with you being gentle to and with yourself and then to your kids. It is a behaviour that needs awareness and practice. If I can get it, you can get it.

3.
SHARING FOR CHILDREN

This chapter is an alternative theory on how teaching children to share correctly can positively affect their adulthood.

Teaching your child to share is important, but helping your children with sharing from a point of view of awareness can also help them to be confident, secure and empowered teenagers and adults. It can help them to be less materialistic, help them hold their boundaries and help them feel free to give to others without undermining themselves.

But before you can teach a child to share, you first must give the child confidence in ownership. A child will only feel safe in offering its belongings to others, when it knows 100%, without any doubt, that the parent will retrieve that child's toy or belonging whenever they want it back. No matter the effects on other children or those children's parents. This is key. The child needs to feel secure in its ownership of its belongings before they feel safe in sharing.

When you put adult pressure on a child to share, you start creating a good child, bad child dynamic. The bad child does not share; the good child does share. Stop and think about that for a moment. Is a child that shares a good child? Is a child that does not share a bad child?

The child that is forced to share grows up and becomes an adult who feels bad for not giving in to what others want, even if giving in is detrimental to their own personal needs and wellbeing. The adult has thus been programmed, at an inner child level that they are bad for not sharing and giving. Because the inner child belief is established at an early age, it becomes a subconscious process whereby the adult has no control over that programming and will freely and openly give too much of themselves.

They might struggle to hold personal boundaries, which in turn can make them feel disempowered, insecure and out of control, just because they are trying to be the good child. They might not feel confident enough to stand up for themselves because deep down they are programmed to believe it's bad not to just give-give-give. Because they have been forced to share as a child, they do not know how to control, or to consider, what is right for their own personal needs. They have been taught by their childhood that it is good to give away their power.

A child's brain will only be sufficiently developed to understand the concept of sharing from around six years old. When you try and force a child of one, two or three to share their belonging you end up just overwhelming their brain. This causes confusion and creates insecurity and uncertainty in the child. This is why the child cries when they are forced to share. Their brain simply cannot understand their parent's need for them to share.

Why is this? This is because what belongs to the child feels like a part of the child itself. When the parent gives the child ownership of an item, the child will take the item into their energetics, and so it becomes a part of them. The parent has given this item to the child, and when we force the child to rip it out of their energetics and share it, we teach them to give away parts of themselves without self-consideration.

We do not wrong the child for not knowing how to walk when they are a baby, but we wrong the child for not knowing how to share when they have not yet developed the consciousness and mental capacity to share.

What do you do instead? Start to show your child that their belongings belong to them and that without their specific permission you will not allow others to take control of those possessions. That even if it is their sister, brother, friend, a stranger, cousin, father who wishes to play with their belongings you will protect your child's ownership and you will protect their belongings even if it makes other people unhappy.

Do this and you'll be teaching your child to trust you, to feel they are safe with you. You also teach them to set firm boundaries and confidence in themselves and how to hold their power. They also learn that their needs can be met and that their desires and passions are important. They become more open and more relaxed about sharing, as well as feeling safe in their family environment.

For those parents who have two or more children, when you allow your child's belongings to be protected, even from the younger needier child, then you are, at the same time, saying to all the children that they are not allowed to take other children's belongings without permission. You install honesty and respect for other people's belongings, you install deep trust in the children that you will always protect their belongings, and you install a belief that you are aware of all the children's needs and that you are present with your children. If you force a child to share, you create sibling rivalry, and you disempower one child and empower the other. You create disharmony and uncertainty in where each child stands in the family environment. The home may start to feel unsafe if their belongings are not being protected. They do not know where they stand and where they are safe. Their belongings become more important than they are.

Case-study:

Two-year-old Amy wants to play with four-year-old Paul's building blocks.

Paul is very protective of his blocks because, he is at that very moment, very focused on building something.

Amy comes over and starts to take one of Paul's blocks.

Paul very quickly takes his block away from Amy and she begins to cry.

Mum comes to see why Amy is crying. 'Come on Paul, you have so many blocks, let Amy have one.'

Paul refuses.

'Paul it's important for you to share with your sister!'

Amy is now crying even louder.

Paul is still refusing to give up his personal belongings.

Now Mum is getting very irritated and is projecting that Paul is a bad boy for not sharing

'Paul, you have hundreds of blocks, give some to Amy to play with "right now"!'

Paul still resists, hoping his Mum will see it from his point of view.

Now Mum is angry and disappointed in the bad behaviour of Paul. He is being a naughty boy for trying to hold his boundaries.

Paul gets taken out of the room and put on the naughty stair.

Paul loses his power: his toys and his flow and Amy gets all the blocks she wants.

Now put yourself in Paul's space:

Paul is happily playing with his blocks. He is creating and developing his mind, his skills and his creativity.

Amy, being younger, is attracted to this flow and comes in and interrupts this space.

Paul wants to keep himself in his flow and does not want to be disturbed because being in flow feels wonderful to Paul.

Paul takes back his block, whilst trying to protect and hold his flow. Paul is instinctively trying to create a boundary to protect his flow and his power.

Amy sends a crying signal to Mum that she is not happy, she wants to also be in flow. Paul's flow feels wonderful and she wants to be a part of it and she thinks the blocks will help her get there.

Now Mum comes in and only sees it from the crying child's point of view.

She does not realize that the small little block is very important to Paul, it's part of him and his flow. It does after all belong to him.

She undermines Paul by wronging him for not sharing. Paul learns that if he does not give-give-give he is a bad boy.

Mum empowers Amy and teaches her that crying will get her more power and that being a drama queen is beneficial.

Paul learns that it's not safe for him to be in flow and he becomes nervous and angry around his sister because she will always get his belongings. He will always have to give away a part of him to make other people happy.

Paul loses some of his confidence in his mum

Amy learns that she can get whatever she wants.

Paul is the bad child in this dynamic

Amy is the good child in this dynamic

Paul's attention span has now been affected. He does not feel safe to totally focus because his home environment is not always seeing and meeting his needs.

Paul has learned sharing is more important than him.

For the parent it does not seem such a big deal to take a small toy from one child to make another child happy.

It's just a little toy, but to the child's undeveloped mind this is undermining, overwhelming and feels like betrayal. They feel like they are constantly failing because their needs are not getting seen or heard. To Paul, that toy is a part of him. And at four-years-old giving up his toy is like giving away a piece of himself. Paul could become afraid of creativity and starts to feel unsafe in his own home.

In this scenario, Mum could easily sit down on the floor next to Paul and ask him softly and kindly if he would be happy to choose some of his blocks, the ones he is not using, for Amy to play with. And if he needs those blocks back she will get them for him.

If Paul is not willing to give up his belongings, then his mum would then need to tell Amy that right now Paul is playing with all of his blocks. She might get a chance later, she might not. But in the meantime, it is up to Mum to take the time to recognise that Amy might be looking for parental direction. Mum could introduce something else for her to focus on. Maybe crayons or play dough.

Paul will feel heard, protected and will deepen his trust in his mum. He'll be developing his skills in focus and he'll be extending his attention span. Amy will learn everything her brother is learning, plus she cannot expect to get everything she wants all the time. Mum will learn that Amy was in need of direction. Both children are learning to communicate their needs correctly.

If it did feel OK for Paul to share his blocks, and he offers several blocks for Amy to play with, then Paul is feeling heard. Paul is feeling his needs are being protected and that his mum is on his side, as well as his sister's side.

Paul is learning how to set his boundaries firmly but gently. Paul feels safe to connect with his sister and knows that his mum is there for him and for Amy too. As Paul reaches seven or eight years old, he will have such confidence in his mum that he will share without fear because he has faith that his parents understand his needs.

Amy has learned that she too is getting her needs met and that it's OK for her to also set boundaries like Paul did. She will learn to respect other people's boundaries and will learn huge amounts from her older brother. If Paul is feeling secure and confident to get his needs met, his boundaries protected and his belongings owned she will be learning this too.

Ownership and Sharing In Public

I remember being in the park with my son. We had a sandpit bag in the car so whenever we go to the local park we have all his sand toys ready for him.

The looks I would get from other parents when I said no to sharing his toys was comical. The amazement and judgment because I was not pushing my son to share. Yet, at the same time I was telling him that he couldn't have other children's toys without permission, because they did not belong to him. I was also teaching him to protect the ownership of other children's belongings.

He was learning that it's wrong to just take other people's things and he should not expect to be given everything he wanted. As an adult, I am sure he will go on to learn to respect other people's belongings and that theft is wrong. In my view, if you are going to allow other people in a park or in a restaurant (or any other public space) to define how *your* child should behave, then you are teaching your children that society defines them. And the danger is you end up creating robotic children. Fuck society's limited beliefs. Instead teach your kids to be free, caring, loving and independent adults. It will create a far better society for them, your grandchildren and their grandchildren.

My final word on this subject. Please do not bow down to society's peer pressure. Peer pressure that says children who share are good and children who do not share are bad. When your child is confident with ownership they will automatically learn to share openly, but only once their brains have developed sufficiently for them to conceive of the concept of sharing.

4.
Fifteen Minutes a Day Keeps the Disconnection Away

One of the most common traumas I have come across in my healing practice is one of disconnection. By this, I mean clients who are disconnected from themselves and disconnected from other people. They don't know how to easily connect deeply to people, even people they have known for a long time. I believe this is a learned behaviour, learned from loving, but very busy disconnected parental upbringing.

In our average everyday lives as parents we are always busy. We are getting the kids up, we are dressing them, feeding them, shepherding them off to nursery, school or college, we are rushing off to work, rushing about for whatever needs doing. We pick them up and we take them to after school activities, we rush them home, get their dinner ready, get them ready for bed and then we start all over again, and we do this for years and years and years. Of course we have holidays together and spend time with the family on weekends, but how much of our time is properly focused on real connection with our children, never mind connecting and gathering ourselves?

In your day-to-day life, if you look carefully, your kids may not be getting enough significant caring, connected, and focused one-to-one attention from you. It's even harder if you have more than one child or are a single parent. Your children may go for months without having real caring connected attention from you and neither of you may notice it at first. But over time, this widens the connection between the parent and the child. It can create a sense that being isolated and living your life in a drone-like robotic kind of existence, is normal.

The saddest part of all this is that your child will most probably get more focused attention from you when you are frustrated and angry with them. Anger and frustration will stop you in your tracks; nothing else counts other than getting your point across and you will focus that force of your anger or frustration at your child. This is an obvious fact. This happens, no need to beat yourself up over it, it happens, period. But if your child is not getting much caring focused attention and they only receive the anger focused attention, then you are training your child to seek negative attention and this could create all kinds of struggle in your child's future.

I am not saying you should *not* give your child anger focused attention. They need that too. They need to see it's OK to be angry, they also need to see how to get over this anger and move on from it. But if it's 90% angered attention and only 10% caring attention then there's the possibility that you are creating a problem for them in their adulthood.

You might read this and say, 'I am paying my kids focused caring attention!' And I ask you are you certain?

I am talking about the attention that is focused directly on the child. Are you present with yourself and your child, whilst you pay them attention? You are not distracted by another child, you are not stressed about work, you are not cooking or cleaning or texting or rushing or driving. It can be hard to step out of life's struggle for fifteen minutes and have some connection. But if you do find this a struggle, isn't it time to deal with your own stuff, so you can connect with your kids?

Single parents, or parents with more than one children, will tell me there is no time for that. Who will watch the other child or children? I believe it's totally acceptable to say to the other child or children something like, 'hold on for five minutes, I am working with your sister'. This is a super wonderful lesson for them. You are saying out loud, to all your children, that you are available for them. You will hold space for them and no one, not even your siblings, are more important than them. But remember, if you say five minutes, then after five minutes, do what you said you would do. Do not end up letting them down, because that way you are using 'give me five minutes' as an excuse to disconnect from them.

I believe the minimum direct focused one-to-one time your child needs in his or her busy life with you is at least fifteen minutes a day. Fifteen minutes of truly listening to what your child is saying about their play and about their feelings. Maybe it's an opportunity for you to offer a story from your own life that relates to what's going on for him or her. If you are busy cooking and stirring the gravy whist you are talking, you are not paying them the attention they need. Your attention and your energy are focused in yourself. Totally connect to you and then them. Be present with them. Meeting your child, seeing your child, hearing your child.

Can You Actually Focus on Yourself?

This is where being the centred parent is so important. If you cannot hold your focus for yourself, then you will struggle to be able to do this easily for your kids. The nice side of this is, as you try and give them fifteen minutes, you are also giving yourself fifteen minutes a day. We all have good and bad days. Try not to be so harsh on yourself if you are having a bad day and cannot focus on your child or children. But remember to make it up the next day. And if most of your days are bad days, then you have must just find that space no matter what, you all need it.

How do you create this focused attention with a child? With younger children, you could get down on the ground and build some blocks with him or have a tea party with her. You could make it practical, like bringing your child into the cooking process when you are making dinner or even bringing in the older child to help change the younger child's nappy and focus on what is happening with them in that moment. You could have a project together or a game you like to play together; my son and I often play backgammon or crazy eights card game together. We also like to take two equal sided tubs of building blocks and see who can build the best ship or car with them. The activity is irrelevant, it's the time spent creating caring, connected, focused time together that counts. It could even be just holding your child after they have fallen and just being with her as she cries, no judgment, no fixing, just being with her.

My favourite time is lying in bed with my son at bedtime and having a chat or a giggle about things that are going on for him. Or, I tell him stories about my childhood. Your stories are always, always better than any book you can read.

With older boys, it's often good to get involved with their play by asking them what it's about or get them to teach you about it. Getting involved with older boy's play will also teach you much more about your sons than just observing. Boys also like aiming and target games. We have kids' crossbows with suckers on the darts, and we see who can shoot closest to targets we have put on the kitchen doors and windows.

I also like to incorporate connected time with cooking, so will often do pizza dough or bread. Both my seven-year-old son and fourteen-year-old daughter like to get into the dough and knead it and punch it and slap and roll it and then make their own pizzas. I use everything organic so they are also getting good quality food as well as connected time.

For babies, a good caring focused time is nappy changing time. As often as possible when changing a child's nappy, take your time, have a play, a giggle, have a cuddle and be present with your child. Nappy time is extremely important. I believe constant rushed or stressed nappy time can cause long-term insecurity around genitalia and intimacy. If you are often stressed or disgusted about nappy changing, then the message you send your child is that your child should be stressed or disgusted with genital intimacy. But if nappy time is a good time, a fun and loving time, then long-term the child will feel confident with their genital intimacy.

Sometimes those fifteen minutes just require you to be present with yourself and to be totally absorbed in watching what your child is doing. You can read to them. I have a friend who still reads books to her children to this day, even those who are grownups! It's a special bonding time between them all. They are a Danish family and she reads the books in English to improve their language skills, that's real multi-tasking.

My favourite connected moments with my son are when we are watching a television program together, something we both enjoy, and he will end up sitting on the arm of the chair I am sitting in and lean against me. Then we get lost in the show together. We are doing the same thing at the same time and we are connected in that process. We connect like that when playing with remote control cars, when playing cards and backgammon. We do it with our special handshake. These are all little moments of connection that we have learned to have with each other. When it gets disturbed and our day stops us from having these moments of connection, we both feel and miss it. It's like the fuel that feeds our connection.

Fifteen minutes a day of focused connection with your child could give you and your child a new lease on life, now and for their future. Can you afford not to?

5.
DEALING WITH CHILDREN'S EMOTIONS

As parents, I believe it's our job to teach our children about their emotions. It's not just our job to make our children happy. Many parents invest huge amounts of energy, money and stress into making sure their children are happy. Why are we bad parents if our children are experiencing sadness, or anger or hurt? Should it not be OK for our children to be angry with us? Or to feel fear or frustration within their young lives? It's our responsibility to teach them how best to deal with *all* their emotions, and how to process them, I do not believe it's good parenting to wrong or dismiss a child's emotional processes. It is not bad to be sad, it is not bad to be angry, it is not bad to be afraid although it is wrong for your children to be afraid of you!

If we focus on our children only being happy, then the message we teach the child is to seek happiness as a priority. This then creates a need to constantly seek happiness outside him or herself. In short you are asking them to live their lives trying to find all the perfect little things that might make them happy. Happy, happy little disconnected people, happy happy!

A parent cannot be responsible for a child's actual happiness, other than trying to provide an understanding open environment for them to flourish. However, parents often get caught in the trap of feeling like they have to stop the child feeling any other emotions other than happiness. Thus the parent urgently tries to create happiness, at any cost, by bringing in external factors like food, treats, gifts and distractions.

A different way to approach your child's emotions would be to sit in the moment and connect with them. Sit with the unhappy child and hold the child emotionally and physically. Be in the sadness or emotional process with the child, and so teach them how to process emotion, rather than wrong the child for feeling the emotion in the first place and thus installing a need for them to bury emotions inside themselves. Teach the child to be courageous about its own emotions, and not to be afraid to feel, not to be afraid to be human. For a parent to do this, they will also need to be comfortable with their own emotions. To accept they may also get triggered whilst supporting their child through the emotional process. We are not perfect parents, but it's the process of trying and failing and trying again that makes good parenting.

If children are taught only to seek happiness, the risk is that they will eventually end up as emotionally retarded adults. Adults who are never aware of when they are in true joy or contentment, because they are certain that happiness is the only goal. As adults, this results in them seeking happiness in mental or physical external connections. Or they could seek happiness in disconnections, as they try to escape their unhappy world. These might show up in various ways like alcohol, sexual addiction, materialism, and disconnection through addiction to mind altering substances, television and video games. This type of adult has been programmed in their childhood to expect external stimuli to make them happy, thus perpetuating disconnection from their internal selves.

To expect a child to always be happy is to wrong the child for feeling his or her emotions. This again creates the concept of the good child, bad child situation. We are again installing the idea that there are good and bad emotions, instead of teaching the child that all emotions are as important as each other.

If it is bad to be sad, it should be bad to be happy. If it is bad to be angry, it should be bad to be excited.

Parents who often struggle with this are usually parents who have not yet learned to manage their own emotions, or who are unskilled with their emotions and so cannot deal with their child's emotional process. These parents need to start doing emotional self-development so they can become more emotionally balanced people and more emotionally balanced parents.

Please be aware, I am not saying you need to wait till you are perfectly emotionally stable before you can have children! I doubt that state even exists, but I am suggesting that any work you do on yourself means you will grow as a person and as a parent. We are all just primates trying to understand ourselves in our own cryptic emotional symphony.

Managing Anger

It's so easy to get angry with our children when they get angry or emotional. Now flip this the other way; you get angry with your child because they are angry with you!

Being ANGRY with a child for being ANGRY or SAD or HURT makes no fucking sense and is totally incongruent. Your child is learning that it is bad for them to be angry, but it's OK for you to be angry. But your child is only showing you what you have shown them. You have taught your child to behave in this way, so you are responsible for this behaviour. Therefore, you need to change so your child can change.

Is it wise to raise a child in the concept of do what I say, not what I do? You are their role model. The role model who is telling them not to trust their role model! I can be angry, but you can't! What happens? The child learns it's not safe to stand up for their beliefs. Do what I say, not what I do is, in a manner of words, just teaching a child to be strongly judgmental.

Give Love, not Food

It's easy to use food as a way of making our children happy when they are sad. It's a known and trusted method. Babies cry, we feed them. But your children are not babies any longer, and they need you to feed them with emotional nurture, not just food. We want to fill them with love and understanding, not food and drink. As well as treating your child to a cheap ice cream, chocolate, sweeties or crisps, you're also putting them at risk of possible food intolerances and diabetes. Treat your child with love and nurture not poisons and materialistic stuff.

It's easy to wrong our children for feeling hurt by referring to their hurt as silly or stupid because as an adult we do not consider that the child's brain is not adult yet, and that what hurts them may be silly or stupid to us, but is very, very real for them.

No matter what emotion your child is experiencing, it's the parent's job to be there with them so they do not feel alone in the process. Even if the child is angry and thrashing out, even if this puts the parent in physical danger, the parent still needs to hold a safe space for them. A parent can hold a safe space for a child even if it's from a distance, or another room. (This is a last case resort though). The space needs to offer love and acceptance for what the child is feeling and going through, even if these emotions are scary, confusing and dangerous.

At a later stage, when the situation has calmed down and normal communication is re-established, the parent can communicate with the child calmly and to the point. This is the moment to tell them that you love them, and you talk about what they were feeling. Create boundaries and directions that the child can learn from. You can both then try and work out why that situation happened, and how to sort out the underlying reasons so it does not happen again. In this scenario, both the child and the parent take responsibility for the emotional outburst without wronging either person. If you try and discipline the child, especially while they are in the moment of out of control emotion, they will feed off the attempt to deal with the situation and it will most probably drag it out longer. This is not a process of ignoring your child. Ignoring your child is simply abuse and neglect.

Of course, it is not acceptable behaviour for the child to thrash out and hurt people in their anger, but it is OK for them to feel their anger. It's important not to wrong the child for feeling what they are feeling. You can work with the child to change the way they react, and how to express those emotions. When you accept they are going through something, no matter what it is, even if it challenges you, do not wrong them for being hurt, scared or uncertain. Hold them.

The Naughty Step

With younger children, if you use the naughty stair approach and leave the child on the naughty stair on their own in their extreme emotion so they can repent for their sins, you are abandoning the child in their emotional state. A state they cannot possibly be old enough to cope with, so the child has no choice but to withdraw and hide their true emotional selves from you and the world. If you go into anger and rage at the child as a means to deal with the child's emotional outburst you are using fear and attack as a means of dealing with their emotion's, and they will either wither away or learn to use fear and attack in their adult lives.

When your child is sad, angry, frustrated, hurt, fearful or in any emotional state, and you acknowledge the child and teach the child that their emotions are OK this allows them to be emotional human beings. This will create deeper truth, and connection between the child and parent. But, like I said before, the parent needs to be able to deal with their own emotional responses to be able to do this for the child.

To raise children into healthy adults, working on your own emotions and wellbeing is essential. You will not get it right every time. You will fall apart too. You will probably have to go back and apologise for not getting exactly what is going on for them. But you will grow from your children. None of this is bad or wrong, but if you communicate this to them whilst it's happening or go back to them and tell them you got it wrong, and then make it right, you are in fact teaching your children that we are all human. We all make mistakes and we learn from them. This way, you bring your children closer to you.

I remember shortly after my thirteen-year-old daughter moved in to live with me full time. There was this particular moment when both her and my seven-year-old son needed me at the same time. So, I just stood up and said 'stop'. I took a few breaths and I was honest. 'I have never had to deal with two of my children's needs at once,' I said. 'I am struggling to deal with it, so let's slow down and deal with one at a time.'

With total honesty, I told them what was going on for me and I brought them into the situation I was feeling. By doing this, I taught them that it's OK to communicate what's going on for them, because I was willing to do it as well. I then worked with them slowly, one at a time, to get to a win-win situation. Everyone is heard, and everyone is happy enough with the outcome, even if that means their needs may not be dealt with immediately. They both got heard and so did I.

Dealing with younger children's' emotions is just to be there with them. Tell them it's OK to be angry, it's OK to be sad, it's OK to feel jealous. To do this you need to also understand that there are no bad emotions, and that every emotion has duality with positive and negative effects on us.

What do I mean by this? Happiness feels good when they are in it, but it also feels bad when it seems to have ended. That's why they cry when the parent wants to go home but the child is having fun. They are losing a connection to their happiness and contentment. This is normal.

Sadness feels overwhelming, but we feel refreshed and lighter after it's processed.

Anger overpowers us, but once it's been processed we are closer to our vulnerability.

Jealousy feels empty but also teaches us what we desire.

All emotions have the can take us on a positive and negative journey.

Being with your child whilst they are in their emotions, and allowing them to flow without your judgment, is a beautiful fulfilling experience for both the child and the parent.

Children who process their emotions physically, by being spiteful or hitting out at others or at themselves, must be addressed. We most commonly wrong the child for this behaviour. But a child can only learn to process their emotions in this way by learning from other people. So, if your children lash out due to their emotional process, then most probably they have learned this behaviour either from their parents, their social surroundings, or from TV. If you are going to be angry with your child for being angry, then the chances are your child is just being angry like you! Put it like this, it's hard to wrong them if you taught them!

You teach your child to tie their shoelaces, you teach your child to read and write, you teach your child to tell the time, but you are also teaching your child how to deal with their emotions by just being you. If you stop wronging your child for feeling their emotions, and you start to openly accept that they and you are not bad for being angry or sad, then you open up a space for your family to process emotion, and to free yourself from explosive situations.

You have to decide what the acceptable behaviour is for yourself and your children in your family, and it needs to be installed strictly and adhered to by everyone. In my home, I like to tell my kids what I am feeling. I am feeling angry right now, or sorry that noise is really irritating me. I use communication as a way of releasing emotional responses. In turn, I ask my kids what they are feeling, and if they cannot identify the emotion they are in, I work through with them what they might be feeling. I will get it wrong but it's a powerful bonding process, and I will stay with them till they have processed it even if they do not know what it was. Sometimes I will allow them to just have space. I am not abandoning them, I let them have their own space and every few minutes I ask how they are doing without expecting them to come out of the process at any time. I am willing to process with them. They are my priority.

Your children may not know what they are feeling, they may just be emotional or seem overwhelmed, but as a parent it's your job to try and read the situation and to report back to the child what you sense they are feeling. It's not a perfect process and you may get it wrong. Often adults haven't got a clue what they are truly feeling, so don't beat yourself up for getting it wrong, it's a work in progress.

To conclude, I would like to share with you what happens when a child becomes emotionally aware.

My seven-year-old son often goes to visit his friend next door and usually comes to check in with me every thirty-forty minutes if I haven't checked in on him before then. But on this particular day he was back very quickly, after only ten minutes. He knew we were going shopping shortly, and that he only had half an hour next door, but still, he was back abnormally early. So, I asked him if everything was OK.

He said his friend next door, who is six years old, had asked his mum if he could come to the shops with us. On previous occasions he'd come with us. But on this occasion, she said no, and when he became emotional and whined about it, his mum said with an angry voice, 'pack it in'.

My son told me he was afraid of his friend's mum and that she was mean and angry all the time. I went straight into understanding his emotions and asked him if he felt uncomfortable when he was next door when his friend's mum was angry. He said yes. I told him it's good that he can tell when he's uncomfortable with a situation and I praised him for coming home to speak to me about it. I feel for my neighbour's son, but I am also thankful for the situation that helped me teach my son how to deal with his emotions.

Emotional acknowledgment is a sign of courage. Teach your children to be courageous with their emotions.

6.
GET RID OF THE NAUGHTY STAIR

I really dislike the naughty stair. No, I mean it, I really hate the concept. Everything in life has some kind of duality, polarization or yin and yang, but the naughty stair's duality is like that of a torture chamber. One-side gains, the other side loses, and unfortunately the side that loses is the child. The naughty stair is for bad, disobedient, a emotionally ignored child to learn to submit to the disconnected, ignorant will of a parent.

The naughty stair is a place of isolation and humiliation. A one-sided space where a child has all its choice, all its power and all its faith in the parent stripped away. It's a place where they are forced to accept they are bad and that they are the problem. It, to me, is simply the family's home torture chamber. It serves to create separation and disconnection from the family and from a child's inner-self. A separation, which will only expand as they mature into a need to punish one, and others, for not obeying what they deem, is correct behaviour. It also encourages children to beat themselves up for feeling and expressing themselves. A trait, which again, can stick in adulthood.

Negative adult behaviour related to forms of punishment, like the naughty stair, can cause adults to deal with situations without knowing how to make a choice for themselves. They do not feel heard or seen and thus never get their needs met. They find it difficult to stand up for their rights and are afraid of their bosses and/or any person in a leadership role. They allow injustice in their lives. They do not know how to be genuine with their emotions and struggle with true empathy. Extreme cases can cause them to be very controlling and violent. At the furthest end of the scale, they also learn that if they say sorry they can get away with anything, and that going to prison would not be a true form of punishment. It's just a place to wait it out until they can be an attention seeking naughty adult/child again.

The naughty stair is a safe way for overwhelmed parents to deal with children. The parent has been taught in their childhood, usually from their own parents, what society expects is right and wrong. These expectations then define their behaviour and thus themselves as either good or bad.

Putting a child onto the naughty stair defines them as bad, and they will only be good if they fit into the need of the parent. It teaches the child they will not be heard, and to bury their emotions, which in turn creates internal hardship, anxiety and physical and emotional dis-ease which they will have to deal with later in life.

Parents need to be aware there are NO naughty children, just children whose parents do not understand their own children. If your child is being """" naughty"""" the child's naughty action should be a signal to the parent that the child is in need of something that the parent is not aware of. There is something going on with the child they do not understand. Rather than the naughty stair, what's needed in this situation is for the parent to gently connect with their child and to help them through their struggle, to teach them how to deal with future struggles similar to this. They don't need punishment and isolation, which only creates even more overwhelming uncertainty in them.

Before placing your child on the naughty step, it's worth asking yourself these questions: Why is your child misbehaving? Why are they screaming? Why are they fighting? These behaviours should be an important signal to the parent that the child is not getting their needs met. The child is feeling overwhelmed with the lack of emotional direction and stability, and they are screaming out for a parent to connect, guide and help them. It's the parent's responsibility NOT TO WRONG the child or the situation, but to use this opportunity to connect with, learn from and re-educate the child through a gentle, loving and understanding connection.

If your child is misbehaving see it as an amazing opportunity for you, the parent, to connect and learn from your child. This in turn creates an essential lesson for the child to treat themselves with gentle loving care, rather than punishing, isolating and wronging themselves. It also brings the adult and child closer together.

The hard parental truth to swallow is that if a parent is punishing a child, it is because the parent believes they too deserve to be punished. This kind of person will always struggle to be gentle to themselves, never mind being gentle on the important people in their lives.

Parents see a positive side to the naughty stair when the child has finally understood and said sorry for their behaviour. But, very often the child doesn't even have the capability to understand their behaviour and why they have been bad in the first place. What frustrates me in these kind of situations, is the ignorance of the parent. Rather than the adult trying to understand what is happening, their default reaction is to just blame and wrong the child. The parent is not parenting, but just being a police state parent.

In most cases with the naughty step, the child learns the parent's happiness is more important than theirs. And by the same token, they learn they do not get heard, seen or understood.

The chances are that the child has no idea why they have acted in this way, and are unlikely to be even aware of the lesson being learned other than 'if I sit here for long enough, I will be let out of this isolation and disconnection torture space for what ever I did to make my parent unhappy.'

The child has learned to feel content in the belief that they are the bad-child. More than that, they have learned it's good to be bad. Being the bad child means that my Mum and my Dad have no choice but to connect to me and pay me the one-to-one attention I am so desperate for, even though that attention wounds and scares me. The child has learned that any connection is good, even the violent connection of being picked up against your will and man-handled and over-powered onto the naughty stair. This becomes good attention, so the parent has taught the child that violence is acceptable. That it is OK for them to be overpowered, that it's OK for them to have no say in their own life. What you are going through only counts as good if it does not challenge the parent.

The naughty stair teaches the child a way of being disconnected-connected. Disconnected to parents, family, friends and society. The naughty stair has become my friend because I am bad and naughty. Playing up, screaming and hitting means I get to be violently dis-connected-connected too and put on to my friendly cold isolating naughty stair.

So, the naughty stair perpetuates negative attention seeking behaviour!
The naughty stair perpetuates negative attention seeking behaviour!
The naughty stair perpetuates negative attention seeking behaviour!
The naughty stair perpetuates negative attention seeking behaviour!

Which stair is the well-behaved stair you use to praise your children? Do you have a space you take your child when they have spent all day playing nicely, without any parent challenging behaviour? Or is it only best to connect with your child when they are naughty?

How about changing the naughty stair to the cuddle stair? When your child is being "naughty" go and take your child to the cuddle stair and sit with them on your lap and give them a cuddle, love them, talk to them, hear and feel what is going on for them. Take time to learn what's going on for your child. Their behaviour is your responsibility.

Even if what's going on for them challenges you, does not fit into society's ideas of behaviour and is causing family upheaval, understand that your child has a reason for their behaviour. They are not just doing it on purpose, they did not wake up this morning and plan to be naughty because there is no cognitive aware process going on for them to be naughty. There are no naughty children, only parents who do not, or are not, willing to understand their own children.

If their behaviour is not aligned with your needs, they are asking, screaming, crying out for your help. It is your job as their parent to try to hear and understand them. Just spending time not being angry or frustrated with them, but listening, hearing and loving them, gives them the option to learn to be calm in the face of life's hardships.

Your child is a mirror of you. If you are not hearing them, they will not hear you. Yes, you will probably have to make it up as you go along, and you will get it wrong-wrong-wrong, but in the process of this you are also being present and connected to your child. This then teaches them to feel safe with being themselves with you, it's not important if there is right or wrong going on, it's the process of connection that matters. The more you hold your child in the challenging moments, the more you get to know your child and the more you will understand your children and the more you will understand what is going on for them. They will help you grow in yourself, that's their job for you. As long as you are courageous enough to connect with your child and not punish your child.

A client came to see me because their child of three was not sleeping, was always fighting, was never obedient and was constantly after sweets, cake and ice cream.

He had recently started kindergarten and the teachers found him impossible to deal with, he would not listen or sit still. He had already been labelled a naughty bad boy by the teachers, and thus by the other children and their parents.

They brought him to me to 'fix' his badness, find out what was 'wrong' with him.

As they walked from the front door of my studio to my healing room, I noticed this bad boy had an obvious and severe difference between his left leg's movement to his right leg's movement as he walked. Once seated, I enquired how long his walk had been so severe. His parents looked at me with total emptiness and said they had never noticed he had a problem with his walking. I showed them the difference in length between his left and right leg. I showed them the uncomfortable position he lay in when he was on my healing couch, I showed them that his issues were not behavioural, but most probably skeletal and muscular, and that he was probably always in some level of pain.

For the first three years of his life his parents had never paid enough attention to how their own son was moving. He simply did not fit into the behaviour they expected, and he was brandished the bad troublesome boy.

After further treatment with a qualified skeletal therapist his walk improved, but more importantly he was out of pain for the first time in his life. His hips were so severely out of alignment at three-years-old, that I believe they'd been that way since birth. He had no other frame of reference other than pain and had got used to being in pain. When he tried to sleep his body could not relax, the muscles were so tight that in bed his pain increased because he was so stiff, so he was sleep deprived as well as unseen, unheard and alone in his pain.

After his initial session with me and his session with the skeletal therapist his behaviour changed overnight, as soon as his hips were aligned he was no longer in pain, which meant he could sleep properly. In turn, his behaviour improved drastically, he could focus on things for longer and his ability to communicate with the family improved. He was now allowed to not be the bad boy.

Have you ever just watched how your child walks? How they sleep? Have you spent any time being deeply present with your child in their body? In their emotions and in their personality? How well do you really know your children? Or, are you too busy being the practical parent, to observe them, watch them and connect with them? If you haven't, then what's the point of having children, if you are missing out on how awesome they truly are and sharing with them how awesome you most certainly are.

These days, I find connecting to my children very easy, but at first, I didn't. My parents were emotionally clueless when I was growing up, and they only showed me one prominent emotion, which was very loud anger. This was something I really didn't want to replicate with my children. So, how I started to connect to my kids, and my clients, was to imagine I was them. Sometimes I even imagine stepping into their bodies, and I allow myself to feel what might be going on for them.

Recently my son, who is seven-years-old, had been going through a period of time where he would seem to get stuck in his sadness, and he would start to cry and could not stop. He would even say he wanted to stop being sad and he would try and stop crying, but he could not and no amount of connection from us was working to soothe his sadness.

These outbreaks are typical of the type of outbreaks, which commonly trigger parents into getting overwhelmed, confused, angry or hurt. Eventually most parents would wrong the child for this irrational display of emotion, and put the child on the naughty stair, or punish them.

But I wondered what was really going on for him to be so stuck in his sadness. I waited for the next time it happened so I could experience it with him. It did not take long before one of these expressive situations came up again. Whilst he was triggered in his trauma I visualized myself gently stepping into his space. I was in a non-judgmental, open-minded space set to explore and to feel and I just allowed myself to get a little glimpse of what he was feeling.

I was surprised to find he was not sad at all. What I felt whilst I was visualizing myself in his space was a sense of anger. He was feeling angry and had no way of understanding anger. To him it was just a huge emotional explosion that resembled one that he did know; sadness. And sadness meant he must cry until he got heard, seen, understood and nurtured. His subconscious mind just reverted that unknown feeling into something that it did know, sadness and tears. As his parents we know how to deal with his common tears, but our normal methods would not work on this emotional explosion because it was not a common release. We were not acknowledging his anger.

So, I took this information and started to educate him about anger. I said to him: 'Harry, I can see that you are not really sad, I can see that you are feeling angry and hurt by this. Harry it's OK to feel angry. It's good to be angry, Harry as long as you try and not hurt other people when you are angry.'

I then explained to him why it was OK for him to feel angry around the situation that triggered him. He quickly felt better, and we moved on and left that experience in the past. But Harry's subconscious had learned a lesson and we had added a layer to his knowledge of emotional intelligence. Harry learned about his anger. He learned it's OK to be angry and he learned how to let it out, and he also learned that his parents are always there for him.

The way you deal with your child's emotional releases makes all the difference. If your child's naughty behaviour is bad, then you are teaching your child that they are bad, and they are wrong. But if you see it as an opportunity for you to learn about your child, and to educate your child, then you are teaching your child to be an emotionally intelligent and confident adult. I do not see how you cannot afford to put more time into their behaviour and not less. Get rid of the naughty step and start being a connected parent.

Kill the naughty stair and create the cuddle stair.

7.
How to Say No to Your Children Without Creating Trauma

As parents, it can be tough to know what to say to your child when they're in that powerful child energy of desperately wanting something. In our very materialistic and sugar-based world, our children can become desperate for what seems, to an adult, to be unhealthy, silly or not worth it stuff. My son would cry in anguish if I said 'no' to him going to the charity store to purchase some slightly broken toy that he would play with for five minutes to satisfy his brain's need for expansion and experience. At first, I found it so difficult to say 'no', it's only a tiny little bit of money, but a year later I have a house full of plastic yucky broken things that he does not even play with any more, but knows he has them, so I can't just throw them away.

Then it was the ice cream. We treated him to ice cream and in turn we programmed his body to crave it. Next thing I knew, I was struggling to cope with the constant pressure of having to buy him ice cream! When we leave his school to go home, I could make our way home by turning left or right. If I turn left there is a shop that sells ice cream, if I turn right there is a shop that sells ice cream. Every time we got to the junction, automatically he is asking can I have ice-cream? Can I have ice cream? He pushed his need for ice cream straight at my heart, to him at five or six years old that need for ice cream was as real and powerful as anything and it consumed his brain. In fact, it became almost a life and death situation for him. His primal brain sees ice cream as life or death. That's because a child's body is hardwired to look for the highest calorie food it can find, to provide as much growth for his body as possible. It's in his DNA. And because we no longer live a primitive life or death life, these small things have replaced the survival need and thus ice cream, sugar and quick fixes have become important to us. Let's face it; the chances of him being taken away by a lion or wild dog are rather small in our western society.

This internal desire for him became a struggle for me. I kept falling for his survival needs, needs that are programmed into my DNA to give survival to my family. So, either I was the good Dad by giving him what he wanted and reacting to his primal survival need, or I was the bad Dad for not giving him somewhat toxic sugary ice cream just before lunch. The struggle pursued for months before I spent some time working out what was really happening for me, and how I could deal with the situation. My five-year-old was controlling me and I was struggling to maintain myself in a harmonious conscious way that would be best for both of us.

Firstly, I noted that the want for ice cream is 100% real. I could not wrong him for his want for ice cream being so strong. I was there the first time he had ice cream, heck I paid for it, and to be honest I kind of like ice cream just as much as he does.

I am not going to wrong him for his want of ice cream. Tick

But that still left a conundrum. How to deal with this real primal pestering to get his wants and needs met? Was I going to ignore him? Not a chance, we raised him

with attachment parenting, so if I ignore him that could be really traumatic for him. Anyway, I am 100% sure ignoring a child is abandonment and emotional abuse. So, I won't be doing that.

I am going to positively acknowledge his want for ice cream.   Tick

But what is the right thing for me to do as his father? I want him to be fulfilled in his young life, and I want him to learn to get his needs heard, seen, understood and met. If I do that, he will learn to hear his own needs and to fulfil them for himself when he is an adult. But, if I give in and give him an ice cream, he's not going to eat a healthy lunch, and he's going to be drugged up on sugar, which is not fair on him at all.

I need to make a choice: his immediate happiness or his long-term wellbeing. The answer seems simple but in the moment it's difficult to see the long-term future and for him the future is five minutes at most at his age.

Why am I struggling at all? I am the father, I am the dad, and I am in charge. What I say goes so why is this a struggle? It's a struggle because I love him, because he is important to me. Because I love him, I want him to be fulfilled and have a 'fucking' ice cream! That is what his survival brain needs right now, to be fulfilled.

But, because I love him, I want him to be healthy, and because I want to be the best Dad I can be for him, I am in this struggle.

So, what do I have to do to be the best parent I can be for him? I have to hear him by acknowledging his want. I have to keep in contact with him and be aware of his long-term wellbeing. I have to recognise and accept his need. I have to educate him and be compassionate to his primal survival, and I have to do all this with love and gentleness

So, this is what I said to Harry:

'Harry, I can hear you want ice cream. I also love ice cream, but because I love you, you cannot have ice cream right now. It's lunchtime and I do not want to ruin your appetite. Ice cream is full of sugar and is not good for you.'

I have acknowledged his need, I have identified with his want, and I have created a firm and fair boundary and given him a good reason why I established the boundary. And I have also offered him a life lesson about sugar and been clear about why I have chosen not to give him ice cream. I

have shown him that I have heard, seen and understood him.

I also said this:

'Harry, because I want to be the best dad I can be for you, you cannot have ice cream right now. You know ice cream is full of sugar and is not good for you. I have the homemade fruity ice-lollies at home. You can have one of those after lunch.'

I identify to him my understanding and reason; I create a boundary and then a lesson on sugar for him. I acknowledge his need and offer a healthier alternative, as well as another lesson about eating his lunch first. I have heard, seen and created a learning boundary experience for my son.

Very quickly after starting that process, he stopped asking every time we got to the school junction. Occasionally, I would stop and buy him ice cream and he would be super surprised. Then I would tell him, 'because I love you, Harry, you can have the ice cream, but you can only have it after you have finished your lunch.'

These are all great phrases to use:

Because I love you, we can not do that.

Because I want to be the best Dad, or Mum I am going to say no to your need

The answer is NO, let me explain to you why I am saying no

However, and this is a very big HOWEVER, as a parent, if you abuse the truth behind your words and use these words to manipulate your kids, they will become meaningless. These are important words. Be the genuine best Mum or Dad you can be and offer your love clearly. Please do not abuse them.

It's important when you use these words that you are open and honest about the reason, even if it's selfish and incongruent. Do not be afraid to say to your child something like, 'I am sorry, but because I love you I do not want you to go to that party. I am afraid of what might happen to you, it's my fear, I know you want to go, but I am not sure you and I are ready to go.' This is fine. These words are reality. Your child may feel hurt but at least they will have the real reasons and not be left hanging. Being gently honest with your kids is so important.

Trauma can be very easily created in children, and every time we say no to our children without explaining to them why we are saying NO, we create a micro trauma, a place in the child where they have no direction, no security and no connection with the parent. The NO you cannot do that, or have that, or play with that, can create a cold sharp space between the parent and the child.

Now, of course, it would be impossible as a parent to go through the entire life of a child without saying 'no'. But, the 'no' that is being repeated over and over again, without explanation or understanding, will start to create defined trauma in the child.

It's important to remember that what we find insignificant as parents, the child might find extremely important, interesting and exciting. Like how the child prefers the box the toy came in, rather than the toy itself. The box, to us, is just a box, we have seen thousands of them before. But to the child they are a space that things go in, they have corners and moving parts and bends, and they can play hide and seek in them. Please do not wrong your child for being inquisitive. Be very careful what you say 'no' to, and what your fear is or isn't. Remember, the little things can become big things for children.

Besides, I love it when my son wants to play with the box instead of the toy. It gives me an opportunity to get to the toy first.

8.
EXPECTATIONS ARE LIMITATIONS

Are your expectations of your children stopping your children from developing, learning and expanding themselves?

As a parent, it's essential to be clear about your expectations for your children. Make sure what you expect for your children is clearly for their highest of good, and not yours. Make sure that it is not *your* fears, childhood trauma or repetitive patterns which are putting your own personal expectations on your children, just so you can cope. Try not to keep them in a space which may be more comfortable for you, but which limits their development. Make sure you also inform your children of your expectations, (as soon as they understand what you expect), so they know where they stand. Unsaid expectations are self-sabotaging time bombs.

It's tough to differentiate between what is right for you and what is right for the child. No matter how good or bad your childhood was, you cannot raise your children the way you were raised. You must, of course, hold some of the morals you grew up with, but a large amount of what was not acceptable when you were a child is quite acceptable now. Our world is developing too quickly for us to try and raise our kids exactly the way we were raised.

Most of us were raised without emotional awareness in a very expectant and judgmental society consciousness. We were taught that girls become Mums and secretaries and men go out to work and become accountants and builders. Women must submit and men who cry are weak. But these days, thankfully, things are a lot different and we simply cannot raise our children to believe girls are weak and boys are strong, or Dads are emotionless, and women are powerless. Or, if we do not fit in, we are bad. If we do not obey we are wrong.

With female clients, the most common belief I need to clear out of their subconscious is that boys are strong, and girls are weak. Boys are better than girls. Boys are more important than girls. Thousands of times I have had to help women overcome these types of childhood instilled beliefs. Beliefs instilled into girls and boys, by mothers, fathers, families and society. We, as a progressive humanity, must not allow this to continue. We simply cannot raise our children with the same expectations as we were raised with.

So, what is it you expect from your children? Do you expect them to behave? But how does a child's brain understand an adult's expectation of good behaviour? The answer is, they cannot. They simply cannot understand what you expect of them. When you tell a three-year-old to behave him or herself, their brain simply has no clue what the hell you are on about. When, in fact, it's probably you

who needs to behave more like a parent. Be less disconnected from your child because you are expecting your
child to know what is appropriate when they simply cannot.

You need to gently repeat and repeat the expectations
over and over again, without expecting your expectations
to be met until the child's brain develops sufficiently to understand you and then still they may not be met. So, you
can get angry with them, and shout at them, but the child
will not remember to clean up after they until they are
seven-eight years old and then still won't because they are
children. As frustrating as it is, I have learned to laugh at
it. I have learned that when my kids are at their friends'
houses they are very well behaved. This shows they are
learning, but when they are at home, if I am going to use
love and not fear, I am going to have to accept that I'll be
repeating myself all the time till I am blue in the face, until
one day they move out and then they have the teaching
and training to run their own lives.

Getting angry with your child when they do not fulfil
your adult expectations is, and I am going to be very blunt,
ignorance, and total absolute ignorance.

A child's brain needs to repeat the same things again
and again to learn from them. A three-year-old will clear
up behind himself or herself once they have seen their parents do the same thing consistently. My son throws his
clothes on the floor every time he gets ready for bed. Should
I expect him to remember to put them in the laundry basket? Well truth be told, I throw my clothes on the floor next

to my bed every night when I go to sleep. He learned it from me; I cannot expect him to do it differently until I change.

Are you going to beat and harass and shout your expectations into your child? They are your expectations. The child does not belong to you. Instead, be the example, not a mean and aggressive disconnected ruler. This does not mean that you let your kids get away with everything. It means you learn how to show authority in a calm gentle manner, with confidence and certainty, so your child knows you are going to stay focused on them. They get to learn from you in a safe and assured way, creating an open connection with your child, so you can teach them how to behave in our world, so they can survive in normal circumstances.

I had a client come to see me for some repetitive pain injuries. His story stuck with me. He was brought up in a home where his father ran the family business and his father's expectations were for him to follow in his footsteps. He would go to college and study in the family business, and then come and work for him, just the way he had done for his dad. My client tried to do this, he went to college, did not do very well, but passed, and after a few years of working with his dad, he was unhappy. His dad was happy that his expectation had been met and expected his son would be happy, but my client was not happy.

One day he approached his dad and told him he was not going to continue working for him. It wasn't satisfying him, and he could no longer do it. He had no choice but to find work that he enjoyed doing. That he wanted to do. My client made a rift in his family by doing this. He knew he had broken his father's expectant heart.

My client then got a job at the lowest point of his chosen passion for a career and started working. He loved it, he excelled at it and now twenty-five years later, he runs his own very successful company that earns five times as much as his father's company could ever have offered him. He has repaired the rift in his family and is living his very happy life with his own family.

If he had stayed and kept to his father's expectations, he would have simply been only limiting himself. His father's expectations were only for his father, not for him. Having these kinds of expectations can be ignorant and selfish, as well as belittling for the child.

The parents' expectations end up making the child feel responsible for making the parent happy and not themselves.

Ask yourself these questions:

- How much of your child's behaviours are working every moment of the day to make you happy?
- Does your child startle easily when you walk in on them playing or doing something you would not want them to be doing?
- Is your child constantly asking you permission to do things?
- Does your child find it easy to say no to you and do you hear the NO?

- Is your child's normal behaviour challenging to you?
- Is your child afraid of you?

This again comes down to understanding who you are and what you want for your child. It's OK for you to have expectations, as long as you own them and tell your child, that you own them.

I have a client who has severe OCD and cleans everything all the time. Her upbringing was with a mother who expected everything to be as tidy as possible, manically tidy. Her mother put her OCD needs and expectations onto the children in the family and caused constant stress and uncertainty in the home environment. My client never knew if her room was clean and tidy enough and she grew up worrying about her mum's needs and not her own. She now has constant anxiety about cleanliness. She ended up in such a state of uncertainty that she would use over £2000 worth of cleaning wipes a year just to make sure everything was clean enough. My client wanted to have a child. She wanted to have a family with her husband, but she knew she had to let go of her expectations of her children to be able to meet her cleaning needs. She now has a family, and although she still has strong cleaning tendencies, her two children do not experience this for themselves. They see Mum clean, but she does not put that on her children. She owns it for herself, and amazingly her children's messes, that would have stressed her out beyond belief before she had children, are not an issue for her anymore.

Do you expect your child to be a doctor? Do you expect your child to be a lawyer? Do you expect your child to have a family and children? Do you expect your child to go to university? It's OK to want your children to do good things in their lives, but it's not OK to expect your child to do the things you want them to do. It's not OK for them to have to be something just to make *you* happy.

It's not OK to force your children to live their lives on your terms, and not allow them to have terms of their own. Either they will run away from you as soon as they can, or they will depend on you to make all their choices in life and not have a personally fulfilled life of their own.

9.
ASK YOUR CHILDREN TO RATE YOUR PARENTING

Every six months or so, I take a moment when I am one-to-one with my child to check in with them. Are they content with our relationship? Do they want anything to change? I ask them these specific words:

What can I do to be a better parent for you?

I give my children the opportunity to tell me what *they* feel is helping them, or not helping them, within my connection with them as a parent. As a parent, we can become blind to how we are dealing with our kids. They change, they grow but we may keep treating them the same way. We should learn from our children.

I believe it is our job to guide our children into becoming well adjusted members of society, to encourage them to stand up for what they believe individually and not just do what everyone else expects from them. It's our job to learn from our children, they are our greatest teachers.

Our children will trigger our own unseen childhood trauma, but we must use this to grow. My son has been my greatest teacher of how to love, to be loved and feel love. My daughter has been the greatest challenge of my life. She has helped me to be individual, and to hold a confidence and self-awareness no one else could have taught me.

Ask your children what they need to help them have a stronger connection with you. You are not infallible, you are busy, and you can get stuck in a rut. If you allow yourself to have faith in your children and if you let them feel safe enough to speak to you without any fear of retribution, they will help you be a better parent.

You have to let them say what they need to say, no matter how harsh, and you must not get angry with them. If you get defensive or irritated by what they say, they will learn to never speak up again and just say nothing to keep the peace. If you are going to ask your kids what you can do to be a better parent for them, then you must take what they say seriously.

There are some obvious points to consider. For example, the younger kids will not understand what to say, but in their words, they might be offering you important snippets of help. If a child says, 'I want you to play with me more', then you might realise you are parenting from above too often and need to get down to their level more frequently.

I asked my son at around five-years-old what I could do to be a better parent. His comments were first, more chocolate, more pizza, more cake (he loves his food) and then after about five minutes he said, 'I want to go on more days out with you, Wayne'. He had picked up on the fact that I'd been doing less outdoor activities because of a physical issue that I had. Prior to that, we used to go swimming twice a week but due to schooling and changes in our lives, we had been going less and less. He wanted more father-son time.

By asking him and listening to his answer, he gave me the opportunity to make our connection stronger.

Can you afford not to ask your children?

10.
INSTANT RETRAINING

It's our job as parents to point out to our children when their behaviour is out of line, dangerous or not acceptable in the different circumstances of life. Although we want them to be free to flow, feel and be themselves, there are situations where, as parents, we need to step in. We should not wrong or blame the child, but always gently and clearly re-educate the child's behaviour as quickly as possible.

We do this by saying and meaning sentences like:

'I love you, but that behaviour is not acceptable,' and then very importantly re educate the child by explaining what is acceptable.

'I love you, but that was not the best choice you could have made,' and then give the child ideas of other more appropriate choices.

'I love you, but that's not the best way to do that, let me show you how this could be done, good try though.'

'I love you, but it is never ok to show me your private bits in a restaurant, even if they are hurting you, we can go to the toilet and check that out for you.'

It's important to deal with the retraining as soon as possible. I have had so many clients whose issue comes from a parent who made the child wait to be punished or reprimanded.

'Just wait till your father comes home, he will deal with you.'

'Go to your bedroom, I will deal with you later.'

'I have not decided what I am going to do with you yet.'

A child cannot conceive time the way an adult can, so the experience of an hour of waiting in fear would be equal to weeks of living in total fear for an adult. The depth of trauma this can cause in a child is unfathomable, but if the situation had been dealt with in the moment, it would have become a lesson for the child rather than trauma. This kind of trauma could even contribute to post traumatic stress disorder (PTS.) in children.

Your child is not naughty or wrong. You have just discovered a behaviour that will teach you more about your child or could warn you of something uncomfortable that your child might be experiencing and needs you to focus on. It's an opportunity for you to pay warm caring attention to your child and their needs. And you do this by gentle re-educating.

A child is naturally without any prejudice or racism and very seldom will you find a child that is cognitively doing things to upset the parent. Children are supposed to be exploring their surroundings, pushing the boundaries and expanding their awareness. We call this growing up. Emotionally, they are a mirror of their parents, so often they are just showing you your own stuff, your own fears, your own worries and your own traumas. When you are making the child wait to deal with an issue an issue, which only needed gentle retraining or re-educating, you are putting the child through unnecessary drawn out trauma. This is stopping them from growing, learning and expanding in any normal way. You are teaching them to allow anxiety to control them, instead of using anxiety as a measuring tool of their safety and survival situation.

If you need to wait for another person to reprimand, punish or deal with your children then you are not really parenting your child, you are waiting for someone else to parent your child. I think if you recognise this happening for you, I believe you need to do some self-discovery with a qualified professional.

It should not be hard to gently help your child fit into what is more suitable behaviour, as long as your expectations are reasonable, and you take into account the child's ability to understand your needs.

It could be so easy for you to just say, 'I am not sure of how to deal with this, so let's wait to see what Daddy thinks about it.' Or, 'right now I am too angry to deal with this, let's wait till I calm down and then we can talk about it.'

Communicating with your child in the moment is very important for their feeling of security and safety. If this is hard for you, please seek someone to help you connect to your own issues, so that you do not regurgitate them all over your children.

A client came to see me in her early fifties. She had a constant fear of success, a serious eating disorder, and a big issue with procrastination. Through our sessions we recognised an issue with her father. A fear of her father that we were able to follow very deep into her awareness. She remembered a memory that seemed to repeat itself in her childhood, ranging from five-years-old until twelve-years-old.

If she did not obey her irrational mother in a quick enough time, her mother would reprimand her by telling her; 'just you wait for your dad to come home.' This could happen at 8 a.m. in the morning and she would have to wait nine-ten hours before her dad came home.

Every time a car went past the house she would flinch in fear, and her mum would remind her throughout the day that Dad was going to deal with her bad behaviour. She remembered her shoulders hurting because she was holding them so tight, she remembered scratching at the skin around her fingers to hurt herself and distract her from her fear. She remembered her heart racing in fear when she knew her dad was in the driveway. Her fear overwhelmed her all-day long.

I suspect her mother put her daughter in this state of fear because it made it an easy day of un-parenting, and because her daughter was quiet and not challenging to her anymore.

By the way, I do not believe her mother did this cognitively. I would expect she had grown up in fear herself and was creating a mirror of herself in her daughter was unaware how this was affecting her. It seemed rather normal for her. (As I always say, self-development and discovery helps make better parents.)

Within minutes of her dad being home, her mum would tell him about her misbehaviour, usually making it sound worse than it was, and Dad would call her into his study. He would be sitting there reading the newspaper. His belt would already be off and lying in wait on the table next to him. She would come in and he would ask her to sit down and wait for him. He would read a few pages of the newspaper allowing her to stew even longer before he would ask her to explain her behaviour, which she could not because she had no idea what she had done wrong, or it had been so long ago she could not remember. Then she would be asked to bend over his chair and he would punish her. She remembered that he did not hit her very hard on every occasion, which in turn created more uncertainty about the outcome of her punishment. As she told me the story I could see her fidgeting and felt her fear in her energy system, more than thirty years after the event, it was still 100% real for her.

I know this is a very extreme case but even the smallest amount of time your child is in anxiety or fear could be creating unnecessary trauma for your child to deal with when they are older.

If her mum had been equipped to deal with her as soon as possible after her infraction, at least it would be over and done with. How we educate and re-educate our children as they grow up is very important. We could be creating huge adult issues, teaching our children that they deserve to be punished, teaching them to hold onto anxiety and to be afraid of every action they make.

To me, the most uncomfortable part of this story is that her entire relationship with her father was based on fear. She does not remember a single nice moment with him until she was an adult and he could no longer punish her.

If your child's behaviour does not benefit them, then deal with it as soon as you can, and as gently as you can and move on. This way you minimalise adult trauma.

11.
OLDER SIBLING NOT BIG SIB-
LING

'Mummy and Daddy have got something to tell you. You're going to be a big sister. Mummy has a baby in her belly and in a while, you're going to get a brother or sister and you will be their big sister. You can help Mummy look after your little brother or sister.'

This seems innocent enough, lovely even, but what's the actual message the child is receiving? Let me translate how the big brother or sister might receive this; your childhood is over, and now you have to be a big girl all the time and act like an adult. You are the big sister now; you now have no choice but to take responsibility and help raise your sibling. Big sisters have an important role and if you fail you will be a bad big sister.

As parents, do you expect the bigger sister to be responsible for the new baby? What does bigger actually mean? Are not Mummy and Daddy the big ones? The ones who are meant to take care of the baby? If the child is suddenly the big sister or brother, does this mean they are supposed to become an adult now? If this is the subliminal expectation you are placing on the child, then the likelihood is they are not going to be able to cope with growing up so quickly, and will, even before the birth, start disengaging from the baby and the parents. The child has never been a big brother or sister before, and no matter how many times you tell the child what it will be like, their brain will not understand it. Their brain can simply not conceive this; it is too dynamic and deep for their undeveloped brain to understand.

You cannot prepare the child for being an older brother or sister. The only preparation you can do is to just be confident and open in connecting, hearing and being with your child throughout the process. It will be new for the parents too. If this is your second child, then you have never experienced having a second child either. It will be a new and very steep learning curve, and you have no choice but to accept this and see what happens. Keep your cool, listen to your kids, feel what's right for you and your children. You are going to have to make it up as you go along, ask for help if you can and do your best. But, do not expect your 'older' child to be a big sister or brother, they cannot cope.

You may find this very hard to believe, but I have come across this kind of trauma in hundreds of my clients. Parents, without realizing it, expect their older child to know everything about being a big sibling and to cope with a new member of the family arriving and changing everything they have ever known.

'You are a big brother now. You know what that is don't you?' 'You have been upgraded to big brother and you must know everything about what that means, and if you do not, well, then you are a bad boy!'

Amazingly, parents totally forget that their child is still a child, but all of a sudden, they expect more from them. They expect them to fetch and carry for the baby, to give up their toys and belongings for the baby and to fit in with the baby and obviously they should love the baby straight away because it's their sibling. Because this is your sibling you should love her. You must immediately love this new living creature, a creature that is suddenly absorbing a huge amount of your time you also need from your parents. And if you do not love them straight away, you are a bad big sibling.

Of course, there is no pressure on the big brother or sister, none. It's lovely being a big brother or sister, isn't it? Or, would it be better to be an older sibling who is still recognized as a child, who will be freaked out when the new baby arrives, who has no idea how to behave and how to deal with such a big change in their parent's lives.

And the parents are surprised when the older child starts to be angry and threatening towards the newborn. They might start acting like a baby because baby acting gets more attention. They start having tantrums because they need to get the same attention they used to get, but the parent will then wrong the child for this behaviour. How could they do that? They know that Mum and Dad are working extra hard with their little sibling! How could they be so distracting? (The sarcasm oozes from my veins because I have felt first-hand how much pain there is in my clients. These same clients who have been abandoned because a younger child has come along. And I don't say the word "abandoned" lightly.)

Parents try all sorts of things. Some parents buy the child a dolly, so they get used to having a baby in the house. Common sense here is not very common. How can they expect a young child to know how to treat a living, fragile baby from playing with a lifeless, plastic toy? A toy that can be dropped, hit, drawn on, and does not need feeding or warmth, and most importantly, a toy that has not taken any attention or time away from their time with their mum and dad.

Are you as frustrated as I am? You cannot teach a child to be a sibling before the sibling is born. You will simply have to make it up as you go along, and it will not be easy, and you can stress as much as you like over it, but that is the reality.

You cannot put the pressure of raising a child onto any child under the age of fourteen. Children under seven will not cope with being put under so much stress over the expectation of their parent to help parent their younger sibling. In this scenario, it's safer for the child to pull away from the sibling and find safety in isolation, or to push away their own needs and turn into a robot that has no choice but to give away its power to the parent and the baby.

If you have no expectations for your older child to be a parent or help you parent, then your child will feel safe joining in to help. It's totally normal for a mother to ask an older child to help with raising the younger child, but if the older child says no, the parent should accept the 'no' and not expect or demand assistance. If you cannot raise your children on your own, you simply should stop having more children. This doesn't mean it does not become teamwork. I have seen many clients full of trauma because they were raised in big families, but I have also seen many clients who have such an amazing bond with their many siblings because it was a team effort. The parents did not expect any help, but they made working together fun and exciting, and they created a family bond because they put no pressure on the kids to help each other. Everyone was an individual, everyone was allowed to have good days and bad days, each child was unique and there was no expectation for the kids to parent each other.

Just this morning, I saw a client full of fear and anxiety with physical pain all over her body. The doctors cannot help. She is one of ten siblings born in a ten-year period, and her parents used fear and violence to control them. There is no family bond and there is no unity. It was just each for their own survival as they grew up.

As a parent, you need to make 100% sure that you are not expecting your children to raise each other. You must insist on each child having their own space and time with you, and they must be brought into unity with the parents and siblings caringly and kindly, no matter the circumstances. To do this takes parents who are willing to grow in themselves. You can give a child space even if that child is in bed with seven other siblings, all you need to do is hear them, see them and understand them, and whilst you are doing that, you teach the other children that they can get that too.

My daughter is fourteen and my son is seven, she loves to bath him, wash his hair and boss him through the cleaning process. At his bath times I ask if she wants to bath him because I know she enjoys it, but if she says no, I respect that. NO is NO. See how this could benefit a child that if they say NO even the parent respects it.

Respect your child, do not expect from your child.

When you have a new baby do not expect your older child to raise your baby for you.

12.
TANTRUMS

Firstly, a child's tantrums are a learned behaviour, learned from one of their parents or one of their siblings. As an adult, you may not think you are having tantrums, but just because you are not banging your feet on the ground, screaming or crying, this doesn't mean you don't emit tantrum energy. You could be energetically freaking out and become irrational, stubborn and forceful in your energy towards your partner or kids and this kind of behaviour teaches your child to do similar. When you are not getting your needs met and you flare out from your own hurt, you are teaching your child to tantrum.

When a child is having a tantrum, it is because they believe their needs are not being met. They are crying out, screaming out for their parents to truly hear what is going on for them. All they want is for the parent to gather them up, and to hold a safe space for them. This helps them feel what they are feeling. All they want is be heard. Take your child's tantrum seriously. It's not a joke, it's not a game to them. They are lost and overwhelmed by their emotional responses and are doing what they have been taught to do to be heard and seen.

They are screaming out in desperation. 'Please help me, please hold me, please rescue me from this uncomfortable unknown feelings that I am experiencing.'

It's a cry for help.

Consider the following statements:

If a tantrum is bad, you teach them that emotions are bad.

If having a tantrum is naughty, you teach them that they are unable to behave.

If having a tantrum is a problem, you teach them they are not worthy of feelings.

If having a tantrum is annoying, you teach them to be afraid to feel their feelings.

If having a tantrum is silly, you teach them not to be taken seriously.

If their tantrum embarrasses you, you teach them to be ashamed of whom they are.

They are begging you to hear them, connect to them and be with them. You do not have to fix the problem or buy them the toy they want. They want you, not the toy, they want to be heard, connected to and understood. Buying or giving in to their needs is not always solving the problem but could rather be perpetuating the problem.

My daughter was 4 years old and decided she wanted a specific DVD whilst we were walking through a shop. I had already bought her a similar DVD, but she wanted this one. I knew that it was overpriced, and like the other DVD, she would watch it once and then never bother with it again. So, I told her I was not going to buy it for her. She flipped out, she was screaming, crying, lying on the floor and thumping her arms and legs in the middle of the store. I did not care what anyone else thought. I simply sat down next to her on the floor and calmly talked to her. I told her I understood that she wanted that DVD, but likewise, I was not going to buy it no matter what. I told her that I knew it felt like she was not getting what she wanted and that it was ok to feel that. But I could not afford to buy her something that was not going to be of lasting value to her. I said she could carry on crying and screaming as long as she needed to and that I would stay with her until she was finished. I told her I was not angry with her and it was OK for her to feel this way. I held the space for her, so she could be emotional, and I didn't get angry with her.

It took a few minutes more and then she was cuddled in my arms. We have never had such an outburst since. Oh, we still have outbursts but mostly she comes to me and shows me that she needs help dealing with a situation, and together we work to get it seen, heard, and processed as best as we can. Every time this happens I believe my daughter feels more heard, more seen, more understood and she feels safer and safer in her life.

When your child needs to have an outburst to get you to hear them, see them, connect with them and understand them, then you have a choice. You can choose to ignore your child and teach them they are bad, troublesome and silly or you can choose to be brave and connect with them. Help them hold what is bursting out of them and whilst holding them, try to help them see and acknowledge what is going on for them as best as you can. Just the trying to hold them is holding them and in turn teaching them they are worthy. You might strike 'out' eight out of ten times in getting to the core of the problem and that's OK. But doing nothing, getting angry or ignoring your child, is for me, simply neglect and abuse. It takes very little to try and hold them. Have empathy for your children. You can never blame them for being who they are, you created them.

If you are able to hold your child whilst they are having a tantrum, but they still cannot let go of their tantrum, then it is very likely you are not connecting to what is really going on for them. Children are not able to understand what emotion is affecting them, which makes it really confusing and disconcerting for the poor parent doing their very best.

So, when your child cannot get over their emotional outcry and your normal method of working with them is not working, change it 'up'. Check what they might be feeling, check how you would be feeling if it was you experiencing this. Could it be anger? Could it be sadness? Could it be that they are hungry or hurting?

Go through the emotions with them until you find something that clicks and fits in for them.

Are you feeling angry because you can't have that?
Are you feeling sad because you feel left out?
Are you feeling hungry?
Are you in pain somewhere?
Point to where it hurts.

There can be many, many reasons a child is having a tantrum and it can be tough to work out which one it is. But you need to keep at it, keep trying and try not to let your frustration get the better of you. I know it's tough. It's easy to say try not to let your frustration get the better of you, but bloody hell it's tough. Even I still have days when I can't hold it in. On those days I say something like, 'I am getting really frustrated with this today'. Note, I am not frustrated with them. I am frustrated with the situation. I do not blame them for being emotional.

When your child is having a tantrum and you ignore or wrong them for their outburst, then you ignore their cry for emotional holding and help, and the danger is that you create children who become adults who need to have drama, struggle, arguments and disconnection from themselves and their needs.

You create adults who do not know how to ask for help, and who get ignored when they need help. Taking the time to understand and hold your child through a tantrum gives them the belief that they will be heard, and that people take them seriously.

Please be aware that when children are small, they process food energy at a huge pace so when they are hungry their brain simply cannot cope. It goes into desperation and can create a trauma response and the child can go into a tantrum or emotional explosion. So, the first port of call is to always offer fruit, nuts, protein, or wholesome food. Sugary foods are totally wrong for this because they spike the child's blood levels and can bring an even worse reaction shortly after.

If tantrums are regular, I suggest keeping an eye on the timing or situation and location of the tantrums. You might find something external could be scaring them or they are hungry or overwhelmed by the situation.

Remember a tantrum is an opportunity for you to understand your child more deeply and to teach them how to cope with pressure, stress and how to accept their emotions.

13.
YOU ARE NOT A CHILD; YOU CANNOT PLAY AT THEIR LEVEL

No matter how hard I try, I cannot always play the same creative games my son plays. Like most children, he has the ability to lose himself in his play. He has this awesome story playing in his head and he gets deeply engrossed in it. At times like this, he'll often want me to be a part of this story, but I simply am not in his head and my brain can no longer truly get to that level of creativity. Like most adults, I've got so many other things going on in my life, including his wellbeing, so I do not have the freedom within me to totally be in the game with him.

This does not mean I do not spend time playing with him. Instead, I use the time to ask him to teach me what he is doing, to explain to me what he is playing. I make sure I do not judge him. I make sure I give him feedback and I get him to question my play. I ask if I am doing it right, I ask what position I am supposed to be in and on occasion I play out of the rules he has created, to challenge his mind and to open up new opportunities for him learn from. Most of the time I only have a glimmer of his true imagination. I can offer some ideas but am happy for them to be rejected. Just being with him is what counts. Just trying to reach up to his amazing imagination level lets him know I am there for him, even if I do not understand what's going on for him.

It's the interaction that makes a difference. Ask your kids to bring you into their play, ask them to teach you, give you a job to do. Do not pull away because you can't understand what is going on. Do not suddenly reach for your mobile phone and sit in the play area being in the way. You do not have to stay and play for hours, but just interact in the play and allow them to have rules and ideas of their own even if those ideas make no common sense to you or science.

Too many times I come across clients who, as adults, now hold back their creativity because their parents couldn't understand or would judge their ideas when they were children. Help your children be creative by engaging with them as best as you can.

14.
Close the Door Behind You, Close the Door Behind You, Close the...

Close the door behind you, close the door behind you, close the door behind you, close the door behind you, close the door behind you, close the door behind you.

Sounds like a familiar instruction?

So how come if you tell your child to do something, once, twice, a thousand times, they still don't get it?

It's because your child is a child.

Your child's brain does not develop in a rational process. It seems rational enough in the books that observe how the child brain develops. But this is just observation. Children are not textbook cases. I have seen my six-year-old son search for a toy for ages, not seeing that it's right in front of him. On other occasions, I have seen him remember where he put something that he last played with three years ago, when he can't remember what he did five seconds ago.

His brain is a child brain. What we deem important, or what we expect it to understand or process, means nothing.

They are children.

If you treat them like little adults but expect them to be children, then you help them learn to be confident choice making adults. Children learn through repetition, and we cannot decide how many repeats we need to repeat. We cannot even expect to understand what the hell is going on.

As an adult, you need to realise that your child is a child. They may not or cannot yet come to the same understanding as you an adult, they do not have the same life experience as you. That's your job to help them with that.

Many parents expect their child to be able to understand basic simple things and get frustrated when they don't follow instructions. Like remembering to close the back door when they go outside, even if you have told them four thousand times already today, they still leave it open. Why is this? It's because their brain cannot and will not remember it, yet.

It's up to you what emotional scenario you want to create if your child does not follow your instructions. You can create fear, stress and trauma about the door being closed so your child does not want to go outside anymore. It's not what any parent wants to create, but when you get angry, the child automatically goes into survival mode. They will learn that playing creatively and being in flow is unsafe. Or, you can come to an awareness and accept this simple principle: You are supposed to be repeating yourself over and over again! When your child is older they will know to close the door because you have very 'gently' reminded them four billion times in their too short childhood to do so.

You may say to your child, 'Close the door behind you' and they will answer in the affirmative and yet still forget to close the door! You have to try and see it from their point of view.

Johnny has just had an idea. He is going to move the trail he made in the sand under the bush over to one side, so his toy army men can go around the bush instead of having to climb through it. In his mind, this is a wise choice and he is totally into this decision.

He is on his way out to the garden to do this and his mind is focused on getting this right. He is feeling excited about his realization and he is totally lost in this play.

As he steps up to the door he is totally lost in his flow. In the back of his mind, he hears Mum say something about the door and he acknowledges her exactly the same way she sometimes acknowledges him when she is busy. He asks her something and whilst she nods her head, she has not heard him.

He is about to get to this very important job at hand when he is violently pulled out of his flow. He hears a "screech" that immediately triggers his 'flight and fright response'. Anxiety kicks in and there at the door is Mum. She is in her angry Mum mode again and he has no choice but to drop his flow, connect to his fear and prepare himself for a full-on

Mum attack. Mum yells at him about the door. Feeling fright-ened, he cowers and runs up to her becoming ever more fear-ful as he gets closer to her. He closes the door in shame. Turning back to what he was going to do, his heart is racing, his fear and anxiety keeps him trapped in his trauma brain and he has to struggle to get into his flow again. He keeps looking back at the door to see if Mum has released her an-ger or if he is going to still be in trouble. He has lost his flow, he struggles to become re-engaged with his idea and he feels less passionate about his choice. He has lost his moti-vation.

If only his mum had simply called out something like, 'Johnny, Johnny, JOHNNY! Could you close the door behind you please?' Mum has accepted he had not heard her properly the first time, even though that was the thirtieth time that day she has asked him. But instead of triggering Johnny into trauma or fear, Johnny finally heard her, turned back, closed the door and carried on within his flow. Dealt with like this, he would not have been triggered into his trauma response. He was accepted as a boy and would probably be less likely to grow up into an adult who is con-stantly checking if he's doing something right or wrong. Wondering if he will get into trouble for making a choice, and so struggle to maintain his focus and self-confidence

How you respond and connect with your children will affect how they deal with life when they are older. No mat-ter how many times you have to repeat yourself, you have to remember they are children. If you expect them to re-member things like an adult, then it is the parent who is being ignorant and forgetting that their child is still a child.

Yes, it's very frustrating. Yes, it's very easy to get trig-gered into stressing over the door being left open, or the toys being left on the floor, or the clothes thrown every-where, or the toilet seat being left down again.

But you simply cannot expect your kids to behave like you. You must expect them to behave like children, and do not fight it. Just accept you will have to say it over and over again, and then over and over again, and then over and over again . . .

15.
YOUR CHILD IS JUST YOUR MIRROR

A child is the mirror of their parents. What do I mean by this? When you are in a one-to-one energy connection with your child (which should be as much as humanly possible) your child will mirror your emotional state right back at you. The child is organically programmed to mirror the parent. This is a survival method that has two main purposes. Firstly, it keeps them in contact with you so that they feel safe and connected to you, and secondly mimicking you is to learn how to survive in this violent, unsafe world.

This is important for you to remember, because when you witness your child's behaviour, in truth you are witnessing your *own* emotional state being played out through your child.

Let's look at this scenario. What happens in those moments when your child is not connecting with you? By this, I mean when they are not running to you, talking to you, hearing you, and basically not noticing you. She, or he, is distant. Why? The truth is simple but profound. It is because *you* are feeling distant and something might be going on inside you, which is troubling you. Your child is simply mirroring this sense of distance. You may realise you are feeling challenged within yourself at that moment, or you may not. But in either case, is aware not to blame your child for their distance. Instead, use it as an opportunity to look at what may be going on for *you*, before worrying about your child.

In my own personal situation, there have been times when I noticed my son being distant from me. It normally happened after my son had been with his mum for a few days, I would be struggling to reconnect with him, and so he was finding it difficult to connect with me too. In these scenarios, I would take a short moment just to connect with myself, feel what I was going through and allow it to process away from me and then open myself up to my son. Within minutes we were playing or cuddling and being connected.

If your child feels safer in their own surroundings, then at around seven years old, this should begin to change as the child begins to hold their own process. By around nine years of age, they are usually holding their own process but this brings in fears and uncertainty as it's all new all over again.

If there is something about your child that irritates you, then that irritation is within you, not in your child. Your child is simply showing you your own stuff.

If you are a relaxed and easy-going person then your child will show you relaxation and easy-goingness. If you are excitable and skippy, your child will show you excitement and skippiness. If you are full of fear and anger, your child will show you fear and anger.

I find this way of looking at my child fascinating. It shows how I can heal myself, how I can work on who I am, and in return how to become a better parent.

Your child is your mirror. He or she will be mimicking your emotions and state of being back to you until they are eight-ten years old.

Because your children are so dependent on you for their total survival they will show you your stuff. They will play out your unprocessed trauma straight in your face. This is when it's important for you to realise they are just mirrors, and instead of focusing on them, work on owning more of your emotional baggage. One of the worst things you can do to a child is unconsciously leak all your passed unprocessed trauma onto your children.

Own your own shit.

If your child is ignoring you or not listening to you, it is most likely that you are not hearing and seeing your own uncertainty in your situation at that time.

16.
LIFE DEBTS

Your children owe you nothing! No matter if you almost died giving birth, no matter how many hours of labour you were in, no matter how many months you had to stay in bed. No matter how many stitches you had, no matter what happened in your life, or in your childhood. No matter how much it cost, no matter what you missed. No matter if your child was born a girl rather than a boy.

Your children owe you nothing!
Your children owe you nothing!

You are the adults. As mothers and fathers, you are responsible for the creation of the child. You cannot blame your child for anything that happened to you in their lives until well after puberty. You are responsible for that, you are the role model. Your children are simply a mirror of who you are. You cannot blame them or hold them accountable without first looking at yourself and your own actions.

If you feel your children do owe you something, then take a moment to reflect on this. They did not force you to have sex and conceive. They were not there with a gun to your head forcing you to do the horizontal mambo. You did this. Yes, you created the child but there is no life debt. Such a concept does not exist.

Your children owe you nothing!

I said, your children owe you nothing!

Your children do not even owe you respect. Sounds tough, but you have to earn that respect. You earn respect from your children by being respectful towards other people, as well as to them. You earn respect from your actions, not from forcing them to respect you just because you expect it as their parent. (My father beat respect into me, so that means my kids should respect me too. You may be talking about slavery not respect!) If you expect respect, you need to look at how your parents instilled respect into you. Was it earned or was it forced? Then you have to ask yourself the big question; do you want your children to be forced to respect you, or respect you because your actions make them proud to be your child?

I cannot tell you how many times I have had to help adults of all ages realise they do not owe their parents a life debt. Children with a life debt become adults that find it difficult to let go of their parents, or they find it difficult to even be near their parents. Parents who think their children owe them something use guilt and fear as a way of controlling their children.

I noticed that clients of mine who struggle with a life debt often find it difficult to work with bosses or authority figures and will struggle to work in any kind of strict environment. I also noticed that clients with a life debt often do not want children or find it difficult to connect with their children. I also find that clients who have a life debt seek out older partners, to try and find a way of connecting with a parent in a safer manner. They try to heal the pain of having to be responsible for the life debt they perceive to owe the parent.

Your children owe you nothing. They have no debt to pay to you.

Their life is theirs. They have no life debt to you.

You have brought them into this world. You have to raise them and so you owe them safe, fair and aware parenting to give them the space to grow and flourish. They don't owe you, you owe them!

17.
PRE-TOILET TRAINING, TRAINING

This client's story will explain this for you.

A mother and father brought their four -year-old son to me because no matter what they tried, he just would not allow himself to be toilet trained. He was doing it in a nappy or he was holding it in.

Every time they tried to put him on the toilet he freaked out and fought them. It was no longer defiance; it was fear bordering on phobia. It had got so serious, the doctors had to sedate him and given him an enema to release his bowels, so he did not poison himself.

The doctors wanted to put him on medication and had already sent him to get psychological help. Why would parents bring their child to a healer for this behaviour and not a behavioural therapist? Because they thought he might have an energetic attachment or past life issue with the toilet and they wanted someone like me to look into it.

I listened to what they had to say, and I asked them when they'd started his pre-toilet training. They looked confused and maybe you are too. But hear me out. I asked them how often they allowed their son to go into the toilet with them when they went. Both looked shocked and said never. Plopping is private. In fact, the father really had an issue with this. His shiny white throne time was very important to him. He locked himself in the lavatory and no one was allowed to bother him. (I wondered what happened to him in his childhood to create such insecurity for him, but this was not the time to explore that).

Because of his parents' attitude towards the toilet, their son had not been given the opportunity to learn from them about a totally normal human function of 'dropping one like it's hot'.

Instead, they expected him to know something he had not been taught. But he was afraid of the porcelain trough and he had no idea what they expected. What was he supposed to do on there? He didn't know. But because he didn't know, he was then made to feel bad for being afraid of the toilet, and for not knowing how to transition from the nappy. He just ended up rejecting it more and more each time. He simply was totally afraid of this thing we call the loo. And that's because his parents had not given him pre-toilet, toilet training.

In my diagnosis, I advised them to never close the door of the toilet until their son was toilet trained. To go home and let him in the water closet whenever they did their dirty business, to deal with their issues around the toilet and let go of the stress of it all and to teach him by showing him.

I know most parents do this already and dream of a time when they can be alone in the loo, but I think it's important to note. My son is seven and I still am not able to lock the toilet door when I go 'drop my kids at the pool', he still needs access to me even though at this age he seldom comes in.

I remember him getting on his knees at two-years-old so he could watch my chocolate sausages leaving their warm home. I felt very uncomfortable, but he needed to see. He needed to learn from watching and it helped him understand the purpose of the toilet. And my own un-comfortableness of him on his knees watching me 'drop one' is also a lesson for him to learn what is acceptable, and what is not when it comes to other people's poop time.

And do not forget, kids love talking about, discussing and teasing about pooing, farting and peeing. It really is the original humour.

If you are kind, your children will learn to be kind from watching you. If you are considerate, they will learn to be considerate from observing you. If you are often angry they will learn to be angry from feeling your anger. And if you want them to have a healthy toilet life, they need to learn that from watching, seeing, hearing and yes smelling you!

18.
SING ALL THE TIME

This is not one that I learned from a client, but it is a belief I share with many of my clients who have children. From as soon as they are in your arms sing.

Sing anything and everything.
Make it up.
Hum.
Growl.
Make noises

Newborns are used to vibrational noises coming through into the warm safe environment of the womb. It's comforting for them. So, when you are rocking your baby to sleep sing, hum, om, grumble, make noises and breathe deeply. The womb is not a quiet place, so there is no need to worry about being quiet around your baby even if they're going to sleep.

I still sing for my son if he needs soothing at eight years old. It's not very often these days, but he loves music. Music and rhythm really helps bring him into the moment. He sings all the time. He sings when he plays, he sings when he is learning, he sings because he is allowed to have a voice. In my house, at any time of the day or night, you can hear one of my kids singing.

My son and daughter go to a school where the kids, all the way from three to eighteen years of age, have singing as part of their education. Just recently my son had two school friends over for a lunch play-date and, as they built their blocks, the three of them sang a song they'd learned at school. It was really heart-warming just to watch and listen to them.

I am not a good singer. I am simply tone deaf, but I still sung to my kids all the time. (If I do it now I get 'the' look.) It doesn't matter what you sound like! As long as your body is making the vibration of sound it will soothe them.

Sing all the time.

If you need guidance, here are some of the lyrics of songs I made up.

This one I came up with when he was constipated:

A little bit of pushing makes a pooh
A little bit of pushing makes a pooh
A little bit of pushing makes a pooh
Which makes you a little bit happier

This was a driving one:

Driving on the road, driving on the road, go go go go go driving on the road.
Harry go, daddy go, mummy go, driving on the road.
And
Repeat and repeat and repeat and 'yawn' repeat.

When my son was tiny and in the first few weeks of his life, I was learning how to connect with him more deeply and I would become totally lost in my connection with him. I would sing:

You are a diamond, not a ball of fluff.
Just a diamond, not a ball of fluff
Yes, a diamond, a diamond not a ball of fluff.
Ruff ruff ruff.

As I write this, I sit here in the coffee shop and it brings me such a huge smile on my face and reminds me of how wonderful it was and still is connecting to my son.

With my daughter, I would literally spend twenty minutes a night singing her to sleep. And to this day, even at fifteen years old, if I sing her that song it makes her smile. It was our special thing that no one else could do.

I have a special sleep song for her, and a completely different song for my son. And interestingly, my daughter's is in Afrikaans and my son's is a mix of bad Zulu and English.

The song that would soothe my son a huge amount was 'Michael row your boat'. It's a song I know only a few verses of and I would play with the words to amuse myself as I sung. But, when you have a deep voice like mine and you sing from your body, it creates a wonderful vibration. Harry would settle because of the vibration. Many people also use OM to soothe babies.

19.
TEACH YOUR CHILDREN TO SLEEP

Your child has not been born into this world like other primal animals. They do not have an instinct that teaches them survival. We are more emotionally, mentally, and socially complex, compared to animals. As humans, our physical development to fully grown adults takes over twenty years. Most animals take far less than that, and some are even born ready to go.

Your baby does not know how to properly be asleep on its own yet. They have been in connection with your sleep patterns whilst they were in vitro and following the mother's sleep patterns. To the infant they literally are a part of the mother. Then, when they are born they are put in a crib or cot and separated from the mother. Their learning tool, their leader has been ripped away from them and they have not yet had enough experience to know how to shift through the natural levels of sleep. If they are co-sleeping with the mother, then they are close enough to still learn these important tools. To teach your baby to sleep well is to sleep with your baby as close and as safely as you feel safe with.

There is huge fear over co-sleeping with babies as parents could hurt their baby. In the research I have done this very seldom happens to sober parents. Learning how to co-sleep properly is very important, but you do not have to have your baby right on your body, you can have your baby in a basket right next to the bed, or you can purchase a co-sleeping cot that connects to the bed and protects the baby from harm. Keep the baby close enough to you to enable that strong energetic connection so the baby can experience your sleep patterns as they sleep.

Sleeping separately creates a separation anxiety for the child. The baby has only ever known internal connection with the mother and needs repetitive experiences to learn from so they feel safe and thus can feel free to grow and thrive. But, if they are separated for their sleep period from an early age, they can become uncertain and uncomfortable in themselves and do not thrive as they could.

Society tends to have us believe that newborn babies are unaware creatures that just feed, poop, and pee when they are not sleeping or crying. I believe that the newborn baby is as close to energetically perfect as they will ever be in this life. They only become tainted when humanity gets its dirty claws in them. I also believe when babies are born they have the most powerful energetic awareness, more than they will ever experience again in their lives, and thus they are learning more from your energetic intention than your physical intention. How you connect with your baby under the age of three years old is the greatest part of their subconscious mind. If you watch most other primates, you see that the mother keeps the baby as close to her as possible. The baby does not let go of the mother. If she were to let go, the baby would become a snack to some predator and so the mother keeps her baby close by. The baby depends 100% on the mother and believes it is part of the mother. So, when we separate our children from the mother too early on in their lives, we create separation anxiety and insecurity in the child. We must remember that deep down in our DNA we are just primates, we are monkeys or apes.

Many times, I have come across adult clients who have sleep issues. The most common issue is separation anxiety, dating back to when they were babies and were woken up because the parent was angry with the child. Your child's sleep is far more important than you realise. They are growing and developing in their sleep, so protect and secure your children's sleep time. It could be what makes them more stable as adults.

So, be more primate and keep your baby as close to you as you possibly can, for as long as you possibly can, and teach them to be safe in their sleep.

20.
TEACHING YOUR CHILDREN TO LEARN

I cringe with a huge urgggggh every time I hear a parent ask a young child the following questions:

'What is this colour, or what is that colour?'
'What shape is this, or what shape is that?'

The parent has been taught by our aggressive schooling system to think that testing their children is teaching them. They believe that testing is the only way to tell if someone has learned something or not.

Parents think they're teaching the child when they ask them what colour is this, or what shape is that? They think they're teaching the child for the child's benefit. Don't get me wrong, I'm pleased the parent is engaging with the child, but I also believe they're putting huge pressure and expectation on their child's undeveloped learning brain. They are expecting and pushing the brain to learn, but in reality, mostly they're just squashing the child's natural learning ability. Often, this is to make the parent feel happy about their parenting, so they can say that their child is the good child or the clever child.

When you put pressure on a child to learn, you create boxes. The good child box, the bad child box, the clever child box and the stupid child box. These boxes close the child mind down and stifle creativity.

The child, whose brain is not yet developed for this kind of learning, becomes overwhelmed and cannot create a clear stream of learning. Instead, it brings uncertainty into their learning process because there's too much pressure. This pressure stems from trying to make the primary care-giving parent happy. The child becomes afraid to learn because learning has so much fear and danger attached to its outcome. Learning becomes this harsh scary thing, instead of just being the natural process it should be.

It's proven that children learn in the womb. They are born with an accent, babies cry with an accent. Russian babies cry differently to British babies, who cry different to Texan babies. Parents did not put pressure on their baby to learn an accent, they just did. This is because they are hard-wired to learn. It's a survival necessity.

Your child will learn to talk by listening to you and your family. We repeat the same words and hearing the same things over and over again, without pressure, helps a child learn. Their reptile brain, which dominates the brain's growth and development under the age of seven, can assimilate all this information as it creates the subconscious mind. So, if you are putting pressure on your child to learn, then you're teaching the child to be stressed about learning and this stress in learning can last forever. You might even end up creating learning difficulties for the child that will translate into their adult life

But, if you adopt some basic simple ways of teaching your child to learn, without putting any pressure on them, they will find learning easy and natural. Learning this way teaches the subconscious mind during its development time that it's OK to learn, that it's easy to learn and that it's allowed to learn. When there is no overwhelming pressure to learn, this opens the subconscious mind to allow to learn.

I'm pretty sure this will make sense to you. As adults, we know how horrid it is to be under pressure to learn something. It creates stress and it's not a good idea for adults and especially not for children. But, how do you help your child learn without putting pressure on them?

For starters, it's very easy to teach a child colours, shapes, numbers and letters without creating pressure on the child's brain. Instead of worrying about what your child is learning or not learning, you just simply teach through being an engaged, explicit and repetitive parent.

Here are some ideas:

Colours:

'Look at that green leaf! It's so pretty shining in the sunlight. See how the yellow sun shines through the green leaf. You know the sun is feeding the plant through those green leaves? It's called photosynthesis. See how the sunlight makes the leaves look a lighter green when it's shining on it.' (Any age, any information. If you do not expect the child to learn without repetition, you give them the space to learn way beyond their age.)

'Let's go sit at the brown wooden table over there. Look at this table. Can you see the different shades of brown? Here is light brown, here is a darker brown. They make great patterns. Look how this pattern of light brown wood circles around the darker brown knot of wood. That's how you know where the tree branch would have grown.'

'I love the way that orange pattern you just drew looks. I can see a face in it. Let me see what else I see in this orange pattern you made.'

'Look at that red car. I think it might be a new car because it's really shiny or maybe it's just been cleaned.'

'This is the blue book I wanted to read with you. It's called . . .'

'Here is your pink toy dolly.'

'I love that yellow t-shirt on you. It really makes your blue eyes stand out.'

'Here is the red toothbrush.'

Shapes:
'That green apple is round.'

'Here is a square grey box for you to put your toy blocks in. I'll put all the square ones in first, and then I'll do the rectangle ones after. Do you want to help?'

'This is an oval basket. It is made of wicker, wicker is made from a tall plant called a reed and it grows in water.'

'Oh dear, you spilled the yogurt. Hey, look! It's spilled into a shape of a tree. Let's clean up the tree shaped yogurt.'

'Look! The water has made a round droplet.'

Counting:
'One step, two steps.'
'One mouth full of food, two mouthfuls of food.'

Basically, just count everything, but until they are ready, do not try to go above ten. They will let you know when they are ready for more. Do not ask them to count with you. Just let them count with you because it's natural for them to copy you. If they get the counting wrong by missing out or mixing up numbers, just start again without telling them they got it wrong. Just start again and do it right, the repetition will teach them.

Alphabet:

'Look, that's a letter H. Your name starts with an H too. H for Harry.'

'That's a letter B for ball B B B.'

'Oh, look that's a G for goat.'

I really do not believe you need to worry about reading and writing until the child is around seven years old. They would rather focus on singing and speaking. Letters are two dimensional and flat, so the child mind can struggle to understand how they work in their multidimensional open minds. Some children take longer to read simply because they struggle with the simplistic two-dimensional world. We are all different. Let your child develop in their own way. No pressure or expectation.

Just keep telling the child what it is you want them to learn. It's easy, no pressure, just talk in more detail. Take away the pressure of learning and they will learn. They have no choice, that's what their brains are designed to do. Do not get in the child's way by pushing and poking at their brains to learn. The more you push, the more you squash their ability. Stop quizzing your kids, instead inform them again and a again.

Do not make a huge fuss over them when you see them learning. Likewise, do not reward them directly when you see them get it right. If you make a big fuss, you create a need for them to get a reward for what is essentially just a basic human learning skill. The only reward they need is you being engaged with them.

But do say things like:

'Good counting there!' Or, 'That was fun counting together. Let's count those books.'

'Good teamwork when we tidied up together.'

'Yes, that is a red table.'

'Thank you for the orange book.'

'I like the way you see shapes in the clouds.'

'Yes, that is a blue shiny car. I can see a red car over there.'

When my son was about four, I started to wonder how well he was learning, so I would do what I will call the trick testing. I would test him without pressure. We were drawing, and he asked me to pass him the red crayon, so I passed him the green one. He looked at me with amazed eyes. 'No Dad, that's the green crayon!' So, I passed him the orange crayon. He worked out very quickly I was playing, and he kind of rolled his eyes and told me which one the red crayon was. Throughout the whole process, I put no pressure on him.

We would count everything. We didn't ask Harry to count, we just counted. When he was counting well, I would skip out a number and see if he picked it up and he always did. When he was counting higher numbers and missed one out, I would just add it in without wronging him for it. No pressure for him to learn.

He is eight years old now and quite daunted with his reading and writing at school. Let's face facts; English can be a complicated language to learn even at the best of time.

You get taught one grammar rule, but it doesn't apply to all situations. It takes time to get your head around the idiosyncrasies of the English language, and to be honest, most adults do not even know it all. That's why my son's mother, his school and I make it very clear we are not expecting him to learn to read and write until he is good and ready. There is no pressure for him to fit into what society expects from children. It is our responsibility to protect him from this, and to teach him how to cope with it by protecting his brain's development until he is developed enough to do it all himself.

This also applies to telling your children they are silly. Tell them enough times that they are being silly and they will grow into adults who do not take themselves seriously, so no-one else will either.

Tell them to shut up enough times and they will never feel safe being heard and seen as adults. What you say to your children, they will learn. It can backfire on you. So, be aware of what you are teaching your children.

Feed their interests. If your child is interested in building blocks, then spend time building blocks with them. Have enough blocks so they can expand on their ability. If you cannot afford something tell them you cannot afford it, but still engage with it. You can't buy a horse, but you can take them to see horses, or go for a horse ride as often as you can afford. You can draw pictures of horses or get information on horses to feed to them. That way when they are older and they do get a horse, it's easier for them.

You are the person who is responsible for your child's learning ability. Not the school, not your partner or your nanny. You are responsible for teaching your child from your point of view.

No matter what you think about yourself, you will always have good things to teach your children. You have hobbies and passions and you can pass on your knowledge by just being with your children and letting them be with you. Just be happy to be yourself and let them learn from you.

For example, I am very good at chopping vegetables and my son and daughter are both learning how to cut vegetables like a professional chef. Obviously, I keep an eye on it as it's dangerous, but they are learning a skill that not many people can learn. I am the one that can help them with that, and because they are doing it, I help them improve. I am constantly teaching my kids it's OK to learn.

21.
THERE ARE NO
NAUGHTY CHILDREN

Your child will not be, has never been and simply cannot be naughty, bad or wrong.

This is impossible. Children are just a mirror of you. They are copies of you. They are your little clones.

If your child is doing something that you deem as wrong, bad or naughty, it simply means you are not connecting and understanding what is going on for them. They are doing this to get your attention because something is going on for them.

There are no naughty children.

There are no naughty children, just parents who do not know what is going on for their own children.

These situations give you the opportunity to open up your empathy and connect with your child, to embrace their and your own vulnerability and to experience true connection and understanding. It is also an opportunity for you to learn more about yourself and your child, so they can be heard and seen and understood. This fulfils their primal emotional needs.

If you are getting angry, frustrated or triggered by your child's behaviour then you have work to do on yourself. The question is, are you brave enough? Are you willing to see inside yourself to heal, help and clean your own trauma so you are a better parent and a better person for you and for them?

You are not naughty, bad or wrong and neither are your children.

I cannot embellish this any further. This is a simple but profound statement. If your child does something that you deem is naughty, it is simply a cry from your child to connect with them, and an opportunity for you to find out more about their needs and requirements.

There are no naughty children, just children asking for their parents to connect and be in connection with them, so the child can learn more about themselves.

22.
TALK TO YOUR KIDS LIKE THEY ARE ADULTS BUT REMEMBER THEY ARE CHILDREN

Talk to your kids like they are adults, but do not expect them to understand you like adults. Energetically they will have a knowing of what your intention is, and over time, learn to communicate with you with understanding.

They will love the positive intention of you communicating with them and they will not need negative attention from you.

You need to be aware that your baby is listening, hearing and learning from you on an energetic level from even before they are born. It's important to offer them loving understanding as much as possible, without you expecting them to understand the way the world works, the way you think or even to understand you.

All you have to be is open, genuine and vulnerable in your emotions with your child, and they will learn from you no matter what age they are.

If you are going through a bad time in your life, your children are going through this with you, so talk to them and tell them what's going on. Be truthful.

Share your reality with your children even if there is no possible way they could understand the reality of it. But, as you work your way through your reality, growing and learning, you are teaching your kids to grow and learn from their reality. You are taking them seriously and they will take life seriously. They will take their play seriously, they will take their schooling seriously and they will take their friends seriously because you have spoken to them as if they are worth listening to and worth being heard.

It's important to make this clear: do not expect your child to understand you and likewise, do not wrong a five-year-old for not understanding the complexity of adult life. It's still OK to talk to them about basic stuff. This is not about putting your shit on them. They are not your confidant, so do not tell them about your sex life, do not tell them about that arsehole at work. But it is OK to tell them that you are having a tough time with a man at work and that's why you are feeling sad and angry at the moment. It is OK to tell them how you feel and what you think about things, but make sure, make doubly sure, you are not leaking your unprocessed emotional drivel on to your kids. Remember, your emotions are yours to deal with, not theirs. If you have lots of leaking emotions, go see a friend or a therapist or find someone to talk to. There are many free groups and services you can use online and in the communities around you. You do not need to leak all over your children.

Your children need you to communicate with them, not vent at them. If you need to vent your anger or emotions, then find a friend or an adult. Call a helpline or stand in the shower and have a good shout. It is not OK to take your stuff out on your kids. But it's OK to say to them something like:

'Mummy is feeling really angry right now, but it's not your fault. It's OK for Mum to feel angry.'

'Daddy is feeling really sad right now, it's OK for Daddy to feel sad.'

But try to avoid phrases like,

'Can I have a cuddle?'

'I need a cuddle from you.'

'I'm feeling sad and I need a cuddle, come give Mummy a cuddle.'

Your kids are not there to deal with or hold your emotions. You can tell them Mummy is feeling sad but do not call them over to nurture you or give you love and cuddles. That's your job for them; it is not their job towards you. They simply cannot cope with holding your emotions. If you aren't coping with your emotions as an adult, then how the fuck can your child cope with them for you? It makes no sense.

23.
DO NOT LIE TO YOUR KIDS

If you want your children to be honest, truthful and genuine in their adult lives, then it's up to you not to lie to or deceive them.

This includes all the little lies, even the cowardly lie that says sorry there is no more chocolate left it's all gone. Although, there is some left but you're too afraid to be honest with your child and say, 'I love you, but you've had enough chocolate today, because I want to be the best parent I can be, I need to say no more chocolate.'

I will not even tell my children that Santa Claus is real. I tell them it's a wonderful story, it's fun to believe in and it's lovely for the family, but you will never hear me say Santa is real.

A client told me a story that when his daughter was three years old, they put their big Christmas story into play. They used flour to look like snow from Santa's boots, they had chocolate-coated raisins as reindeer poop, and they had half eaten cookies and an empty glass of milk. They created the fictional fantasy lie of Santa for her, weaving what they thought was needed to make their daughter love the Christmas spirit. They thought this was what good parents do. But in truth, all they did was create an opportunity for a child to experience disappointment and have to deal with it later in life. Christmas dictates to almost every parent that we must do this, it's what society says is right for children at Christmas.

When she woke in the morning they milked it and explained that Santa had been and drunk the milk, eaten the biscuits and you could even see the reindeer poop on the floor. What wonderful parents they were! They were quite happy with their performance for their daughter, and at three she could now truly understand the sparkling magic of Christmas, the most magical time of the year.

A few days after Christmas the family went for a walk in the woods, and whilst walking they noticed their daughter was eating something. In her hand they found a bunch of real dear dropping. Yes, she was picking up real dear droppings and eating them like they were chocolate-coated raisins.

That was a reality check for them.

If you have lied to your children in their childhood, then you have no right to be angry with them when they lie to you. You taught them that lying and deception is what you do, even to the people you love and look after. Your children are behaving the way you taught them, so do not wrong them for your bad behaviour

Tell your children the truth within reason. You can say it's too complicated for them right now, but you will explain it to them when they are older. I have told my son many times this is not appropriate for you at your age. When you are older we can do it together or I can explain it to you.

Be brave enough to tell your children the truth. You can tell them the truth, and then be there to hold them through their reaction. Be with them and allow them to go through whatever they go through, but tell them the truth. This way they learn they can cope with life and they can approach their adulthood with honesty and reality.

You might be concerned this does not create creativity and mystery for the children. This is something I've been told, but again, I am not saying do not do Christmas. I am saying tell them it's a magical story and share that magic with them, but do be honest with them.

If you deceive or lie to your kids, then you are not setting a great example. To be afraid, to tell the truth, just in case the other person cannot handle it, encourages them to be cowardly and to shy away from the truth. They become afraid to be truthful with themselves and to one another, and this stops them from being able to recognise and share when they are not happy. Instead, being honest and truthful with your children, no matter how hard or challenging it is, teaches them to be honest and truthful for themselves and in their lives.

Help them to be truthful and honest by being gently truthful and honest with them. Learn to be genuine and they will become genuine adult people.

24.
GESTATIONAL TRAUMA

What was happening for your mother whilst she was pregnant with you?

This is a question I have asked to many of my clients. What happens to the baby whilst in the womb can define the baby for its entire life. There is proof that a baby is born with an accent and babies will cry with an accent akin to their parent. We know the baby is learning and aware in the womb. For example, the baby's third eye chakra becomes active and connected at about seven weeks, and thus the baby is now in flow with its internal and external energetic flow and begins to learn.

As I write this, I am worried about soon-to-be-mums getting anxious about this subject and worrying they have done something to already damage their child in their adult life before they have even given birth. Let me reassure you, the foetus will ignore day-to-day stress and anxiety. It's only the anxiety that is repeated and intently focused on the baby that can affect the infant.

So, if you have a bad day, or a bad week, or you have a weak moment and wish you weren't pregnant and then the next day you love being pregnant again, then the foetus won't be bothered and will ignore those brief fluctuations. The foetus won't pick up on these quite normal types of fluctuations; remember this child is far more energetically aware than you are. But, if the mother is in a dire situation and this situation is constant and affects the foetus's survival, then over time, this could be taken on by the foetus as a risk and could program the foetus negatively pre-birth. Your baby is far more energetically aware than you are.

Newborn babies will climb from the groin area and make their way up to the breast to feed without any form of help. They are intuitively awake and energetically aware. Newly born babies are not just dumb creatures that we have to slowly educate. In truth, our sole purpose in education is to help them to survive in our unsafe and dangerous world. Energetically and emotionally, they are leaps and bounds ahead of us. They are most likely the closest to God, Buddha, or the Universe than they will ever be again.

Unfortunately, our world can be dirty and destructive, and social pressures are overwhelming for all of us. But fortunately, newborn babies are very clear on their needs and will let you know what they want. But it's up to us to listen and try and meet those needs, so our offspring can survive to carry our genealogical line further into the future. This is why it's essential to start listening to your baby's needs whilst they are in the womb. This means your energetic relationship with them starts before birth, meaning they are totally aware of what is safe and unsafe in their surroundings even before you pop 'em out.

How do you create this energetic relationship with them pre-birth? Firstly, dealing with your personal fears and traumas will help. This does not mean you should not fall pregnant until every trauma is sorted, it means you work through whatever comes up for you and you own it for yourself. Don't ever start telling your baby about how awful the pregnancy was and make your child feel responsible for being born. Your child owes you nothing.

I will list several experiences of gestational trauma with clients. But please be aware these are extreme situations.

One of my clients in her 40's had a very difficult relationship with her mother. She would constantly try to make her mum happy and always try to get her attention. She felt, no matter what she did, her mother just ignored her and no matter what, this situation never changed. She knew there was love there, but the feeling of disconnection was constantly underlying their relationship.

When I asked what was happening for her mother during her pregnancy, she told me that her mum's own mother had suddenly died when she was four months pregnant with her. Whilst her mum was pregnant with her, her mum went into shock and trauma at the loss of her mother and so pulled away from the pregnancy due to external stress as well as emotional trauma. My client had been trying to reconnect with her mum ever since. This information helped her understand her relationship with her mum better.

I had an elderly client who spent most of her life alone. She had a belief that sex, intimacy and love were not for her and she was ashamed of everything about being female. She had an unbelievable shyness and embarrassment about her body and her femininity and dressed, even in her 60's, like she was a man.

When we looked at what was going on for her mother whilst she was pregnant, I learned her mother had grown up in a devout Catholic family and had been convinced that sex was bad, and even though she had married the man her parents wanted her to marry and she was happy to be pregnant, her mum had this awful fear of being seen in public whilst she was pregnant. This embarrassment was acute. She was embarrassed people could see she was pregnant which meant they would know she'd had sex, and even though the sex was with her husband she still felt dirty and ashamed. Throughout the pregnancy and into early babyhood, her mum was embarrassed about her sexual self and so passed this fear onto her daughter, my client. Just becoming aware why my client had these fears and shame helped her to come to some sort of peace as to why she had followed the path she did. It was not her fault.

In my first book I wrote about Alex, who spent the first twenty-five years of his life in a total mess. He couldn't make choices and couldn't decide where he fitted in. During his session, we discovered that during the late stages of his gestation he had been bullied in the womb. He'd had his umbilical cord wrapped thrice around his neck and was being suffocated. His fear of life and choices had come from a situation that had happened to him and not because of him. Alex is now happily married with two children. The trauma in his life happened in his gestational period.

I have had many clients where their relationship with their parent is one of rescuing them, most often created if a mother has had a miscarriage before they were conceived. The mother suffered extreme loss and heartache from miscarrying and consequently, is now afraid to make a connection with the foetus she is now carrying. All the way through the pregnancy the mum is in fear of losing this baby too, so when baby is born the mum feels like she is rescued. During this kind of scenario, the baby picks up on the disconnection and fear from the mum during its gestation, but likewise notices this fear suddenly drops once they are born happy and healthy. As a consequence, the child then energetically believes that it has rescued the parent in some way, and this can create a lifelong pattern.

Once again, if you are pregnant, or have children and worry that you might have influenced your child in some way, please do not get worried by this. But, if you are having issues with your kids that do not make sense, then think about what was happening for you and your child whilst in the womb. This could help you define an issue going on for your child and thus assist you in changing

151

things for the better. There are also many wonderful ther-apists out there that can help you with what you find. It's ok to seek help.

25.
ARE YOUR CHILDREN PUTTING YOUR HAPPINESS BEFORE THEIRS

Do your children feel like they need to make you happy? Do they stop being themselves, so you can feel safe and secure? If they are, is it because you aren't holding your own emotional state well enough for them to feel safe?

A client came to see me with her nine-year-old son. She asked if I could help with her son's erratic sleeping patterns since he wouldn't fall asleep unless he was in bed with her. He tried to fall asleep in his own bed, but something reacted inside of him. But when he stayed at his dad's house he fell asleep easily in his own bed. Could I help with this?

I first enquired how he used to fall asleep before he was seven. She told me she kept him in bed with her because she and his father were having a hard time in their marriage and got separated when he was six. I asked if she had considered if her son was staying in her bed for her, not for him. He might have learned that to keep Mum and Dad happy it would be better for him to be in the bed. Even though his dad had since moved out, he was still in the same pattern and I would bet it's because she got something from him being in bed with her. I asked if he was filling the space of sadness she felt when she got into bed alone. I then asked her a harder question. Was her son an excuse for her not to get into a new relationship? Had she truly dealt with the hurt over her broken marriage? I suggested that her son might be so tuned into her emotional state that he woke up when she was feeling lonely and uncertain. Her son was now her protection from the challenges of moving forward, and dealing with her emotions and allowing a new relationship.

She was stunned at what I said and so was her son. You could literally see the awareness roll down his face as the truth flowed through his brain. He had been wronged for his sleeping patterns, but now he realised it wasn't his fault. In fact, he was doing exactly what his mother needed him to do.

It is never ever your child's fault. It is always the parent or caregiver's issue that is being played out by the child. The nine-year-old was simply trying to keep himself safe, and the best way to feel safe was to keep his mother happy. So, when she went into loneliness and started to connect to the emotions bubbling up about her marriage break-up, he reacted unconsciously to fix her, so he could keep his level of safety comfortable.

When his mum was hurting and entered a place of deep despair, she disconnected from him and he had a sensation of being abandoned. This is why he made sure he was there for her whenever she needed support: when she was alone downstairs, when she came up to her empty bed, when she was tired and unable to distract herself from her unprocessed hurt, he automatically and unconsciously needed to make her happy for his own safety. The session ended with a mother who felt guilty, but aware of what was happening. She now had a way forward, and he felt like he understood himself more and was far more powerful and comfortable with his need to make his mum happier than he was.

Another example I think is relevant for me to tell you is about a family that had fallen apart very early in the child's life.

He was less than one-year-old when his parents realised they could not live together anymore. Being devoted parents they both put a huge amount of effort and support into their child. They both also did absolutely no emotional clearing after the break-up and neither of them had found a new relationship since the divorce.

He was now seven when he came to see me, and the issue was his inability to be away from his parents for any significant period of time. When he was with his mum he desperately missed his dad and when he was with his dad he desperately missed his mum. Mum and dad weren't seeing eye to eye and I suspected there was a competition of who loved him the most running unseen under the entire sticky situation.

Both parents told me how much they had missed him when they exchanged him from parent to parent as a baby. The tears and hurt the poor adults had to endure every weekend when they swapped their son from parent to parent was hard for the poor "adults" to deal with. This was one of the only things both parent agreed on.

I took stock of the situation and explained that because neither of the parents was taking responsibility for their own emotions, this meant their son had started to do this for them. Every single time they'd swapped him over, they created an energy of abandonment in their child. Why? Because the parents were feeling abandoned themselves and weren't doing anything to deal with, or heal, their emotions. Instead, they were both in a 'perpetual pity party' over their divorce. The consequence of not dealing with their own emotions meant their son had taken them on for them. He learned that to make his parents happier he would take responsibility for both of his parents' emotional issues. This is why he went into trauma when he wasn't with the other parent, as he was too busy worrying about them. This worry stemmed from the feeling of being responsible for their sadness – the sadness they felt at having to pass him over to the other parent. This little boy was feeling responsible for both his mother's and father's happiness and unhappiness.

You should have seen the look on the parents' faces when they realised their behaviour.

What about you? Are your children putting your happiness before theirs? If you do not know, then you best find out, and soon!

Do you make them give you cuddles, hugs and kisses because you are feeling hurt or lonely?

Do you let them stay up later because you are feeling lonely?

Do you get them to talk to their other parent instead of you talking to them directly? 'Go ask your father?' If you do this is it an excuse to not have to take responsibility for your parenting?

I remember after my parents got divorced. My father would tell me to ask my mother something for him. I would tell him no. 'You were married to her for thirty-seven years! I think you're grown up enough to give her a call yourself. I will not be your go-between.' Your children aren't old enough to know how to stand up to you yet. If they are being the go-between, stop it and be the grown-up yourself.

When they do something for you, ask them, are you doing that because you want to, or because you feel like you need to make me happy? If they answer yes, I'm doing it for you please refer to the following chapter about being a better parent.

Recently, I worked with a client who found it difficult to finish things in her life, so we went into the energy that stops her doing what was right for her. What we found was her need to do everything for her mum and her dad. They were always arguing about housework and cleaning. Her dad was very strict with cleanliness and her mum would fight with him about what she thought was suitable cleanliness. My client started to clean at about five-years-old, to try and sort out any mess she saw. It was safer for her to just clean it rather than hear her parents argue again. At age five she was stopping herself from following through with her stuff and was taking responsibility for her parents' happiness.

What are you putting on your kids?

If you are putting things on them, then change it quickly and instead communicate with your kids about how proud you are of them for trying to make you happy. But be clear with them that it's not their job. Then, if needed, get yourself some help to understand what's going on for you or for your relationship.

26.
WHAT CAN YOU DO TO BE A BETTER PARENT

You love your children and want the best for them. This already puts you on the right track. However, no parenting is perfect. It is an undefined process that has an undefined ending. You really have little control over the outcome and there is no way to tell how your kids will turn out when they become adults.

Your children do not come with an instruction manual. I know, the minute after my daughter was born, I asked the midwife to go back in and search for it, but alas there was none. You can only do your best. But, to do your best, you need to be at your best as much as possible. What does at your best mean? It's about owning your own stuff as often as you can.

For example, if you are an anxious person then accept you are anxious and do not let it become an issue for you. Instead, learn to own it and not put it on your kids so that way your kids won't have that issue. E.g., 'I'm feeling really anxious about you doing that. I know it's my anxiety, but you don't have to be anxious about it too. Go for it, but be careful.'

If you are a single parent who has not got as much time as you would like for your kids, then make the best of the time you do have. Try not to bring your worries into the time you do have with your kids.

If you struggle with your emotions, then tell your kids you have a hard time with emotions. 'I'm finding this very overwhelming. Mum is not great with emotions, but I can work through it, it's not your fault.'

My advice is to do as much self-development as you can. See a therapist, have healing, have massages, reflexology, learn to meditate. Take time for yourself, but be mindful not to create abandonment or separation anxiety in your children as you take that time.

Teach yourself to express your emotions healthily and in return, your children will learn from you how to express their emotions healthily. Expressing emotion is proving to be a key benefit to healthy, long and stable life. Unprocessed emotion causes impaired cellular growth on a DNA level.

Say things like:

'I am feeling angry right now. It's OK to feel angry.'

'I'm feeling really frustrated with you not listening to me, so let's find a way for us to listen to each other.'

'I can hear you want those toys and I can see that they look like fun, but it'll be your birthday soon. You never know what you'll get, so I am not buying that for you.'

'Let's do this tidying up together so that it gets sorted.'

Express yourself with words and emotions, not through explosions and aggression.

If you can't find time away from your children, then take them with you to a healing session and give them something to do whilst you are there. Have online video therapy in the evenings at home. Join parenting groups, read and feel into everything you can on the Internet. Do not listen to advice, but hear the advice and make your own decisions.

Look at things from the point of view of you and your child, and feel what it would feel like if you were in your child's place.

There are no excuses any more. There's plenty of help and information out there for you. You've got to just be brave enough to go for it. Even if you're just spending five minutes a day sitting with your eyes closed and connecting with yourself to start off with. These little moments will help you become more aware of what's going on for you, so you're not putting your stuff on your kids. Even just five minutes you-time gives you the time to reflect on yourself and own your shit.

I've seen many clients who bring their children with them, from babies up to seven-year-olds. It is very interesting to watch the child go through healing shifts as the parent does. If your therapist won't allow it, find someone else who will.

Here's a great self-help healing technique that you can do on your own. I learned this during my divorce. It's not great with babies but from about two-years-old it's brilliant.

The Shouting Game:

I was so frustrated during my divorce and noticed I would feel even worse after picking my kids up from my not-soon-enough-to-be ex-wife. I needed to vent. I needed desperately to scream. I was so pent-up and would literally boil with emotional hurt and anguish.

But, instead of suppressing it deep inside, or freaking out at my kids and scaring them, or being miserable the entire time they were with me, I invented the shouting game.

We would do it together. It's very easy to do. I would say, 'are you ready for the shouting game?' My stepson was four and my daughter was two

'Are you ready?
One
Two
Three
Deep breathe in and . . .
. . . shout and scream as loud as you like!'

This game is awesome in a car. No one else can hear, but anywhere will do, as long as you aren't going to give someone a heart attack!

We would do it three or four times and then move onto another game. But, I often remember my kids asking me to play the shouting game, because for them it was fun as well as a release.

Breathing in deeply and allowing your frustration out of you during the out breath is a fantastic way of releasing pent-up emotion. More importantly, at the same time, you are also teaching your children a way of releasing their own emotional pains, rather than holding them in. It's a win-win game, other than the occasional looks from people passing by!

To be the best parent you can be, take time to work on your stuff. Grow, develop and acknowledge who you are, the good the bad and the ugly and own it for yourself.

27.
ARE YOU LIVING THROUGH YOUR CHILDREN

Many times, I have come across clients who cannot make choices for themselves. They are not certain who they are, and they have no idea what their life purpose is. In other words, they are lost. Interestingly, when we delve into why they feel this way, we often find a parent who has been living their life through their child. The parent's intention is not a malicious method of parenting, but rather an ignorant unaware process of parenting.

The parent's own personal disappointment and unfulfilled childhood needs are being placed onto their child. This forces unspoken responsibility onto the child, as they are urged to become the healer of either their mum or dad's (or both of their) hurts. The child begins to feel they are responsible for their parents' happiness, and in doing so, will let go of their own childhood needs. In order to be the good child, they just end up meeting their parents' unprocessed childhood trauma.

Wayne Lee

Such a level of adult pressure becomes totally overpowering and consuming for the child. They can lose all ability to find their own path. Furthermore, their personality gets lost because their actions must define the parents' needs of success and happiness in life and not the child's. The child has no choice but to survive. In this type of relationship, the child has no choice; all they can do is focus on what they need to do to survive. This happens because the parent have not yet worked sufficiently on their own development and aren't aware enough to see the outcome of their actions. They are passing their trauma down from their childhood onto their children. This could be called an ancestral shadow.

For the child, having such severe adult need and expectation placed on them usually just ends up recreating the same emotional neglect and disappointments that the parents went through in their childhood. The parent is disappointed because their childhood needs were not heard, seen or fulfilled, but then they go and create the exact same trauma in their child! What they often fail to understand is that by putting such expectation and pressure on their children, what they are really trying to do is heal their wounds through their child.

This sends a message to the child that their life does not belong to them, and that there is no point in ever deciding for themselves. In doing so, they never get to learn how to deal with easy or difficult life choices and this hinders their personality development and their ability to feel safe in their own adult lives.

In my healing practice, I often see adults who are afraid to live their lives in any way that makes them happy. Sounds hard to believe, but it's because they've been taught by their parent that they should not have their own life or make their own choices. When they were children, if they made a choice that made the parent unhappy then they would get into trouble. To the child that trouble is equivalent to death; it triggers a survival trauma and they are then trained to be afraid to live their own lives. Living through your children trains them that their normal life is one of subservience. In a way, a child who has been taught to make their parents happy is no better than a child in slavery.

Here are some examples to illustrate my point in more depth.

Scenario One: Expecting your child to be a ballerina because your parents couldn't afford for you to have ballet lessons.

What a good idea. Mummy can fulfil her childhood disappointment through the child. I love my child so much. I must make sure they're happy because my childhood wasn't happy. The only thing that would have made me happy was to be a ballerina, so my daughter has no choice but to become a ballerina, never mind if she wants to or not. You will do ballet and you will like it, or else you have disappointed your provider of security and safety, leaving you uncertain for the rest of your life. The best part, of course, is that you will end up just like me. Never heard and never understood, and I won't know who you really are, just like my mother doesn't know me at all.

Scenario Two: Expecting the child to be a professional footballer because Dad has an all-consuming passion for football.

Child: Football is the most important thing to Dad. He watches football all the time, in fact, Dad would rather watch football than see me or speak to me. I know, I'll play football, that way Dad will see me. Look Dad! I like football.

Dad: I'll be your coach and we'll work out and practice football every waking moment, even though you're not a particularly sporty child and would rather be doing maths or creating with your building blocks. You make me so happy that you like football, but you disappoint me because you might not become a premier footballer. I know you may only be five-ears-old but we can start doing daily strengthening exercises and see if we can blow out your knees by the time you are twelve. Yay, I'm living through my son.

Scenario Three: I became a doctor because my dad was a doctor, so I had to be a doctor too.

I know you are only two-years-old, but we expect you to go to university and become a doctor. Because we love you and are afraid of change, we want to limit you with as much expectation from as early as possible in your life, because if you become an engineer or a plumber or a designer or a baker, we will have nothing to talk about and I won't be able to control you. This way I won't feel challenged and being challenged makes you a bad child and that is not allowed in my world. You will be a doctor and I think you will specialise in urology just like me. I am so pleased you agree. Now let me change your nappy.

Scenario Four: You'll be the first child in the family to go to university. Hang on, let me also choose for you what you're going to study.

Now, there is no pressure, but you're going to be the first child in this family to go to university. You will prove to every single member of my family that I am special and worthy by you going to university. I can't wait for you to be born so that I can start to create the biggest guilt trip on you! You will have no idea how to say no to me. You will go, but you can study anything you want, as long as it's not anything that means you must travel, work weekends or earn too much money. But anything else that keeps you close to me is fine. That way I can show the family what a good a parent I am because you want to spend as much time with me as possible. No pressure, do what you want, as long as it's what I want you to do.

Scenario Five: You have must learn to colour inside the lines. 'NO! Not like that. Let my OCD side do it for you.'

Here are some arts and crafts for you to do. I know it's only the second time you have used scissors, but you aren't cutting that perfectly straight. Here, give it to me, let me do it for you. Urgh! (Stupid child challenging my perfectionism). While I am doing this, why don't you colour that in for us, but be sure to get it in the lines. Hang on! NO that's outside the lines. We should keep things in the lines, that's why there are lines on that picture of a teddy bear. Drawing in the lines means you will fulfil my OCD. I'm so afraid of getting things wrong that I cannot let you get things wrong. Just leave it, just sit there and don't move whilst I do all the colouring in and the cutting out. You are bad for not knowing what to do and being three is not an excuse.

Scenario Six: You are my lovely little princess. Look at you all dressed in your white frilly dress, going to your friend's third birthday party. Oh, you look so grown up and so lovely.

Now darling, you're wearing your white dress and the party is at the park so you need to be very very careful not to get your dress dirty OK? Later; Mum says; I told you not to get your dress dirty! Now get into your stroller. I'll strap you in, so you don't get any more dirt on your dress. How you look is the most important thing in the world. I know I'll push you to the side of the play area and you can watch your little friends play. That way you'll never feel like you're apart from anything and be too afraid that how you look defines who you are.

These might all seem farfetched, but I have witnessed variations of all the above, sadly.

In addition, here are some more brief scenarios I have come across:

If my child can read by the age of three then I'm the best Dad in the world, never mind the unfathomable pressure I put on my child's undeveloped brain.

I'm the best Dad in the world if my child can run faster than all the other children and I'll be disappointed in them if they can't.

I'm a good Mum if my children are thin. As I have an issue with my weight, my kids must not eat fat, I won't even bother to find out if that's advisable or not. (It's not advisable by the way, the brain is made of fat and fat is needed in every cell in the body, so kids should be eating healthy fat in their diet).

If any of these things seem familiar to you, and you are doing this (or a variation of this) to your kids, then it's time to practice more self-awareness and deal with your own needs from your past. It's not up to your child to fix your childhood or make you a happier person or parent.

If you're unsure, try answering the following questions:

Are you 100% certain your children are telling you what they really feel, or just what will make you happy?

How certain are you?

Have you already, and unknowingly, programmed your children to obey your needs before they feel their own needs?

Are you raising your child how you were raised and how society expects you to raise them?

I know these are hard questions, but they need to be asked.

Let's look at it in a more constructive way. Take this particular scenario involving education – a very common conversation between parents and children. If your child is doing a certain activity, ask them why they are doing it. You can ask them what they have learned from doing their lessons. If they are resisting, and do not want to do the lessons, will you insist they continue simply because education is important to you? If finishing your education was something you didn't do, then are you getting them to finish it for you? Many of my clients stay in dead, destructive marriages because they have this need to finish what they started. They have been taught they don't have a choice to change when things are feeling wrong for them.

I am not saying if your child says no, you must just stop, or they should quit their lesson. I am asking you to discover why your child says no, or why they are resisting something and then work through what is going on for them without your needs getting in the way. I am asking you to recognise when your needs are overpowering the needs of your child, and when they are hindering their development and personality.

My son does not always enjoy his swimming lessons, but he knows he has no choice. If he wants to go crabbing at the seaside and hang off the end of the quay pulling up crabs, then he needs to learn to be able to survive if he falls into the water. There is no choice and he is aware of this. Some things in life we have no choice over, such as paying our mortgage or rent, bills and following the laws of our society. But at the same time, we have so many other places in our lives that we can choose. Teach your kids to choose for themselves even if it challenges you, and then thank them for the challenge because the challenge helps you be a better person and parent.

It became very apparent my son loves to sing. At times his singing and the sound he made would drive me and his mum crazy. So, we came up with a strategy to distract him from singing because two hours of the same short melody and beat can become very irritating. For three years I asked him whether he would like to do singing lessons. He said no. I didn't ask again for six months and then I asked again when he was six, when he told me he wasn't ready yet. Only recently, when he was eight, he decided he would like to do singing lessons. So, I arranged a singing lesson. The day before his first lesson I had a word with him. I told him he could do lessons for as long as he liked, but I said if he didn't want to sing any more then that was fine too. He could stop at any time. If he wants to keep singing, and never uses it for anything but the enjoyment for himself, that's fine. I have made it clear that there is no pressure on him to do anything if he does not want to, other than just enjoy his lessons. Of course, I have dreams and wishes for him. I am only human, but those dreams and wishes are mine. I will not put them on him. That's not fair on him at all.

Here are some other important questions to ask yourself:

Is it OK for your children to fail, fall, struggle and get things wrong? Do you want to jump in every time your child seems to be having a hard time? Do you want everyone else to see that your child is doing well? Are you defining your parenting and individuality through your children's behaviour and success?

Do you put pressure on your children to do well at school? If they do well, do you tell everyone you know because it defines you as a good parent? Do your children want to do well because they know you will be happy with them? Are they now putting themselves under so much stress that they cannot cope?

If any of this is happening in your relationship with your children, then in my experience in my healing practice, this might mean that your children could very well start to procrastinate in life. They are no longer certain who they are living for, and they're not receiving the pleasure of their own success because their success is being used up by the parent.

Now, I am not saying you should not be proud of your child. But you should not only be proud of your child for winning or doing well. You should be also proud of your child for falling, losing and getting back up and going for it again. You should be proud of your child for really being themselves, and not just for their actions alone.

If you expect your child to do well, and when they do not, you feel hurt by this, then you are living through your child's successes. The hard truth is that you are not living the life you should be leading for yourself, and you do not own your fear of getting things wrong. You have not yet processed your own hurt from your childhood and you would benefit from some self-development.

28.
DO NOT COMPARE YOUR CHILDREN

Your child is an individual. Do not compare them with their siblings, do not compare them with their cousins and do not compare them with their friends. And certainly, do not compare them with your childhood or with yourself.

Treat each child with individual respect.

You might be surprised that this happens, but I have had many clients who grew up being compared to their cousin, to their sister, or to their mum's best friend when Mum was a little girl. I have also had many clients who came from a big family, as much as eight to twelve children, and whose parents' excuse was there were too many kids to treat them all individually. I always find that shocking. You did the deed, you had the kids, now you best work harder to make sure that when you deal with them, you deal with them as individuals. Respect each child as their own unique self, or you may create a very uncomfortable environment where unequipped kids are raising kids and it becomes feral.

I met a lady from a large poverty-stricken family. Both her parents worked hard to survive, but every single one of their nine kids had one-to-one time with their parents. In this family, there was respect and there was individualisation, and no one was bullied, there were no major arguments and no aggression. Instead, everyone worked together with respect and care. It is possible, even with nine children, it's just up to the parents to take responsibility and to do more than just get through their day.

When you compare your child to anyone, then you encourage him or her to judge themselves. You make them compare themselves to others.

Comparison is never healthy, not in childhood nor as an adult. All it does is make the adult seek out people they can either put up or put down. Why? Because they're too afraid of people at the same level. People at the same level feel like an uncontrollable challenge to them. When we put a person on a pedestal all we do is put them on a higher standing, which means they are not a challenge to us. When we perceive a person to be below us, then they are seen to be of lower standard to us and so are inconsequential. And someone who we see as on equal standing is someone who could take something from us, and thus becomes a challenge.

Adults whose parents have constantly compared them to others can become judgmental, lonely people who end up feeling either superior or inferior to other people. This is because the parent has repetitively belittled the child through comparing, comparing, comparing! No matter what you expect from your child, no matter how you want them to be, learn to let go of comparing and just go along with the journey of your child discovering who they are. Ultimately, just enjoy them for who and what they are as a unique human being.

Your child is most likely 25% their father 25% their mother and 50% themselves. So, let them become who they need to be. Be their protector throughout the process and most of all, enjoy their individuality.

29.
HOW TO TEACH A CHILD
A LESSON

Without fucking with their security and safety!

What is a lesson?

Is a lesson something that empowers your child for the future? Or, is it a violent process of creating fear in your child, especially if they don't do what you expect of them? This is an important realisation to make as parents. Do you want your child to be gentle toward themselves, or do you want them to be violent toward themselves when they are adults?

I guess it's a bad idea to write a chapter of your book when you've just witnessed firsthand, unaware stupid parents creating trauma for a nine-year-old child. But since I did witness it, let me tell you about it.

I was in a bakery with its own little coffee shop and noticed a family sitting nearby. They appeared to be regulars because the children were really making themselves at home. It's always nice to see children feel comfortable enough in a place that they can just be themselves.

The nine-year-old daughter had brought some jewellery with her from home but left it on a nearby empty table when she went off to play. I then watched her parents take the jewellery and hide it. The mother noticed me watching, gave me a wink and said, 'she always leaves things laying about, so I'm teaching her a lesson.' At first I didn't feel anything was wrong with the situation. Instead of the jewellery going missing or being lost, the mother had taken it to protect her child's belongings. But no. I was very very wrong.

When the daughter came back to the table a light comment was made about where her jewellery had gone, and the little girl started to hunt for it. She must have searched for six or seven minutes before her tears started to flow. She kept on searching, but at the same time, became more and more distraught. And all the time, her mum and dad just sat there and let her go through this quite violent and totally un-necessary lesson. I was horrified. These parents thought that torturing and neglecting their daughter's emotions was a good way of teaching their child a lesson.

In the middle of the searching, the mother was able to lean over to me and say with a wicked little grin on her face, 'she's always mislaying and leaving her things behind.' I was lost for words and so sad for this little girl that I just stared at the mother blankly. If I could go back in time I would hopefully have been brave enough to say to the mother that she was literally emotionally abusing her daughter.

My son will tell he has misplaced his toy; 'Wayne, have you seen my toy?'

'Yes, Harry it's on the kitchen table by the door'. In this scenario, I've told him exactly where his toy is, and he has about a one-meter area to search in. 75% of the time he will not see it. The younger they are, then the more likely their brain has not sufficiently developed these particular searching skills. So, after a few minutes of reassuring him that it's there, I will go find it for him. Most of the time, the toy is right in front of him, but his brain just cannot see it. I remember this happening for me when I was a child, my mother was like the super-snooper, and could find stuff in a second after I had been looking for what seemed hours.

To teach this kind of lesson to your child, prepare yourself to be a tolerant repetitive parent. Just repeat yourself over and again:

'Henry, you left the toy on the table.'

'Sally, please remember to bring your pencils.'

'Bobby, close the door.'

And over and over again!

There is some really obvious science to this. The reptile brain only learns from repetition before it can grasp something as a subconscious process. So, if you want to teach your child a lesson, the only sane safe way is to repeat yourself and repeat yourself.

30.
'WALK' NOT 'DON'T RUN.'

How often do you hear parents screaming commands to their children?

The best place to see this in action is at a public swimming pool. Children are always super excited to go swimming. 'Swimming! YAY!'

They want to run to the water, they want to run around the pool and, as we all know, running at a slippery swimming pool is an accident waiting to happen. Falling on your head near a swimming pool could kill you, so that's why parents all over the world are shouting, 'DON'T RUN, DON'T RUN, DON'T RUN, DON'T RUN!'

And what do the children do?

They run, and sometimes they fall and the parent says, 'I told you not to run.'

A child's brain, actually any brain for that matter, cannot conceive the negative of the word. You can say "don't run" a thousand times and the only word the child will hear is "run". When you tell them not to touch, they touch. When you tell them not to put that in their mouth, they put it in their mouth. When you tell them not to fight with their sister, they fight with their sister. Don't mess right now and they mess. Don't shout and they shout.

So, what do you do? It's simple.

Say what you want your child to do, *not* what you want them not to do.

When they start to run at the swimming pool you say, 'WALK'. Make that connection, 'Steven WALK,' and repeat and repeat.

'Don't touch' becomes 'please leave that alone'.

'Don't put that in your mouth' becomes 'take that out of your mouth, or not in your mouth please.'

'Don't fight' becomes 'play nicely please.'

'Don't mess' becomes 'let's be tidy for now.'

'Don't shout' becomes 'shhh, quiet please.'

These are not the exact wording, as obviously you must use your own natural positive wording. Ultimately, the rule is to say what you want them to do, not what you do *not* want them to do. It's a tough one and you will find yourself correcting yourself many times, but it's worth it in the end.

Think of the effort you put into this as teaching your children to become positive thinking adults who will relate instantly to the positive.

You **don't** have to do this for your children? You **don't** have to buy all my books? You **don't** have to be gentle to yourself? Wink Wink.

31.
IS YOUR CHILD ACTUALLY NAUGHTY

There are no naughty children, just parents who don't understand their children. However, what happens is the parents' own inner child trauma can get triggered by their child, and so they end up wronging their child for being the one to trigger this trauma.

The question to ask yourself is whether your child is truly being naughty, or are they just challenging you? Could they be doing something that children are supposed to be doing, like being children? Is your child actually just being a child?

Is your child truly behaving naughtily?
Or are they just:
  Curious.
  Creative.
  Social.
  Humorous.

Showing you yourself.
Playing.
Learning.
Reaching out for connection.
Being a child.
Afraid.
Happy.
Excited.
Desperate for love.
Awesome.
One of a kind.
A genius.
Emotionally sensitive.
Calling out for help.

If you don't know what's going on for your child, then why the fuck not?

Isn't that your job as their parent? If you don't know what's going on for your child how can you be the best parent possible for them and for you? How can you decide if they are being naughty or not, without understanding their behaviour?

If you are rating your child as naughty, it's most likely because *you* are not connected to your own inner child trauma. Most probably their behaviour mirrors something in you that you perceived as "wrong" when you were growing up. You believe that you were, and are naughty, and it's 110% your shit going on that needs to be sorted out.

Every time your child creates a reaction in you, it's simply a clear sign that *you* have been triggered. Being triggered isn't a bad thing. It's a gift because it creates a wonderful opportunity for you to get to know yourself, and your child better. All it takes is the courage to stop and see why you have been triggered and then to own it.

In fact, parenting in this way, and allowing your children to be your mirror, is one of the greatest gifts of parenthood. But the key is to then be adult enough to grow from it. This all makes being a parent not just worthwhile, but one of the greatest experiences on earth.

So, please see your child as perfect as possible and appreciate all that you can learn from them.

32.
THE FIRST STEPS TO EMOTIONALLY STABLE CHILDREN

When and how do you start instilling emotional stability in your children?

The answer is easier than you think because this is a primal and simple processes that mothers and fathers can do with their babies.

Yes! You start when your child is a baby.

In reality, this starts when the baby is in the womb. If you're in an emotionally stable place yourself, then your baby will start to become aware of that. If you get overly irritated with being pregnant and you blame that on the pregnancy, then you're already blaming the baby for you getting pregnant. Ummmm let's think about that for a second! Yep. So not the baby's fault.

I am not saying you must ignore your feelings around the discomforts of pregnancy. Feeling fed up when you're about to burst, the swollen feet and the constant weird desires and cravings – all these can be uncomfortable. But own it for yourself. Never blame your pregnancy for you being pregnant. See the distinction?

Once it's time to get your bun out of the oven, no matter how that goes, you'll be so happy to meet your little bun for the first time. This is when emotional confidence training for your baby begins.

But, before I explain what that is and how to do it, you have to remember one important fact. Your baby has just spent nine months growing inside of you and for about seven of these months, baby has been aware and been growing more aware every moment. By birthing them, you have just put your child through what may be it's biggest transition of their entire life. Out of the safe confines of the womb, your baby is going to be feeling insecure, vulnerable, uncertain and probably very afraid. And these feelings are going to go on for at least the first three months of baby's life. So, it goes without saying that these first months are when you need to be there for your baby as much as possible.

A client of mine was very pleased to tell me she was pregnant. No! It wasn't mine. Her husband is also a client of mine. A month after their daughter was born they contacted me for help.

They told me how wonderful she was all day long, how well she fed and slept throughout the day. The trouble was happening at night. When they put her to bed at night she began to cry and would scream for hours. The stress of this was so severe that everything was falling apart around them.

I asked them to explore what was happening for their daughter to cause her to be this stressed at night. What we discovered was a sense of abandonment. My client believed that babies go to bed at a certain time and that after this time she could sit with her husband, have an evening together and disconnect from being the mother and father for a few hours before bed. However, this disconnection went both ways. It was something their daughter could pick up on and as a consequence, she felt vulnerable and afraid. In fact, she felt so afraid that she screamed for connection.

Thankfully the outcome was simple. They still sit together in the evening and have their time together, with only one little difference. Their daughter is right there with them, or on them. They do not abandon her and leave her. When I say abandon, I do not mean they were physically leaving the house, but for a month-old baby the energetics of disconnecting with her felt like abandonment.

Be like an ape or monkey, be a primate for at least the first six months. Keep your baby as close to you as possible and keep connected. I know it's hard, and I know having a baby is a shock to your system too, but you are the grown up and it's only for a short while. Hopefully.

So, let's go back to the heart of this chapter: How to teach your baby emotional stability. Are you ready?

When your baby is crying, you show her a crying face, when your baby is smiling, you show her a smiling face.

There you go, that's it.

Wayne Lee

What the fuck you are saying?

That is it? All I have to do is mimic my baby's facial expressions?

Yes, that's it! When your baby is crying, mimic her facial expression back to her for a moment and then pick baby up and soothe her.

How does this work? When you mimic a baby's facial expression you are speaking to your baby without words. You are saying; 'I see you are sad', 'I see you are uncomfortable'. You are showing your baby that you understand she needs something, and that you are there for her emotional self.

You say, 'I can see you', and then you do it all over again, and again, and again.

Your baby can only communicate and connect with you in a certain way. So, you mimic your baby in the exact same way. This way your baby can feel accepted. You mimic the smiles, the farts, the pains and the surprise. You just mimic and love.

That's how you make a baby turn into an emotionally stable child.

You mimic, and you love.

33.
IN FUCKING CONCLUSION

So, here we are at the end.

I have insulted, swore, been sarcastic and blamed my way throughout this entire book, and hopefully you've kept up with me without ending up hating my guts! To be honest, I don't mind if you have ended up hating me, just as long as you've seen parenting from a different point of view. If hating me helps some child become a more balanced adult then I have no problem with that.

Of course, this book wasn't just about parenting. Many of the people who've been a part of creating this book from start to end have made it very clear that even if you don't have kids, and you don't want kids, that reading this book has helped them understand their own childhood trauma and has opened the doors to healing and changing within themselves. As a healer, this is one of my greatest sources of joy.

And as a parent, what makes me truly fulfilled is how many people have commented on how this book is not just about 'how not to fuck-up your kids' but also about 'how to love your kids', and how to gently show them your love.

Before I go, the final snippet I would like to share with you is this: They are babies and kids, so love them with everything that you are, but in that love let them be individuals. Let them help you grow by taking responsibility for yourself, and in turn you will teach them to take responsibility for themselves when they are adults.

Be their guide, not their slaver.

Be there to empower them, not to belittle them.

Let them learn to live their lives on their terms, not only yours.

This way they will grow up to have big happy content lives and is this not what we all really want for them?

Thank you for persisting with me, putting up with my rants and thank you for caring enough about being a parent to reach out and grow.

It's all fucking over now!

I would like to thank my daughter for pushing me to write more than I had intended to. I would like to thank both my kids for being my kids and all my clients who are so brave to come and share their lives with me so, I can help them heal themselves.

Thank you

Wayne Lee
www.wayne-lee.com

CPSIA information can be obtained
at www.ICGtesting.com
Printed in the USA
LVHW100934280821
696162LV00017B/618

9 781999 963040